"Edward Bullmore provides a clearly written and compelling argument for the importance of the immune system and inflammation in depression. This lively book explains a major frontier in clinical neuroscience that is not only influencing research on depression, but also on schizophrenia and Alzheimer's disease."

Steven E. Hyman, Harvard University Distinguished Service Professor, Department of Stem Cell and Regenerative Biology

---

"Professor Bullmore puts forward a fascinating theory that attributes depression to inflammation rather than serotonin imbalance as has traditionally been thought. Whatever the truth this book is a stimulating and interesting read."

Professor Wendy Burn, President Royal College of Psychiatrists

---

"A great read, this thought-provoking book presents inflammation as the major driver of depression. A real page-turner that raises important questions for us all, including how we should practise medicine going forwards and can we restart Research and Development using this paradigm? Highly recommended."

Dame Professor Sally Davies, Chief Medical Officer for England

First published in 2018 by Short Books,
Unit 316, ScreenWorks, 22 Highbury Grove,
London, N5 2ER

This paperback edition published in 2019

10 9 8 7 6 5 4 3 2 1

A CIP catalogue record for this book
is available from the British Library.

ISBN: 978-1-78072-372-3

Illustrations copyright © Helena Maxwell
Cover design by Two Associates

Printed at CPI Group (UK) Ltd, Croydon, CR0 4YY

---

theinflamedmind.co.uk
Animated film made by Nexus Studios

Praise for *The Inflamed Mind*

"Psychiatrists are re-thinking depression. Is depression due to trauma, a chemical imbalance, brain circuits misfiring? In this beautifully written book, Professor Edward Bullmore shows us why we need to look at the immune system if we want to understand depression. This approach not only bridges the mind and body, it suggests new approaches to treatment. *The Inflamed Mind* is an important book, a hopeful book, for anyone who wants to think about depression in a new way."

Tom Insel MD, Co-founder and President, Mindstrong Health

"*The Inflamed Mind* confronts the reader with the converging revolutions in neuroscience and immunology that give rise to a new perspective about depression and its treatment. It traces the roots of dualism, the tendency to view mind dissociated from body, and then calls for moving beyond dualism in order to understand how inflammation in the body affects brain and mind. In an erudite, enjoyable, and accessible way, Professor Bullmore conveys the profound impact of this new perspective by helping us to appreciate the links between traditional 'medical' and 'psychiatric' syndromes and it identifies new anti-inflammatory treatments that may cross the boundary from general medicine to psychiatry."

John H. Krystal, M.D., Robert L. McNeil, Jr., Professor of Translational Research; Chair, Department of Psychiatry, Yale University School of Medicine

"*The Inflamed Mind* is not only a dramatic breakthrough in our understanding of depression. It is an extraordinary exploration of what it is to be human."

Matthew d'Ancona, author of *Post Truth*

The

INFLAMED
M|ND

A radical
new approach
to depression

EDWARD
BULLMORE

℠

List of Figures in Order of Appearance

To my family

CONTENTS

Preface

One of the things that first attracted me to psychiatry, many years ago, was that it tries to deal with the most personal human afflictions: clinical disturbances of our selves, our emotional balances and imbalances, our states of mind and memories, our ideas about the world and its relationship to us. As a young doctor, the richly individual content of mental health symptoms seemed much more interesting to me than physical health symptoms, like ankle swelling or skin itching. It was also attractive to me, from a scientific perspective, that all these mental symptoms must originate from the brain; but it was not yet known how. It seemed likely to me then, and it still does today, that if we could understand more about how mental health disorders are generated by brain mechanisms we would be in a much stronger position to do something about treatment and prevention. We would probably also feel less ashamed or afraid to talk about mental health issues if we knew more certainly where they came from, or what caused them.

So, when I was about 30, finding out more about how mental symptoms originated from the brain became a professional research mission for me. At this time, around 1990, many psychiatrists were focused on how brain chemicals like dopamine and serotonin could cause disorders like psychosis and depression. But it was clear there was an enormous amount more still to understand. I realised that I would need to become a scientist as well as a clinical psychiatrist.

For several years in the 1990s, I was supported by the Wellcome Trust to do a PhD, supervised by Professor Michael Brammer, at the Institute of Psychiatry in London. The first functional magnetic resonance imaging (fMRI) scanners were just starting up, in a few places around the world, and I got involved in mathematical analysis of these new-fangled fMRI data, to make maps of human brain function in healthy people and patients with mental health disorders. I started writing and co-writing many scientific papers on neuroimaging, neuroscience and mental health. This was a very exciting transition for me. I was lucky enough to be in the right place at the right time to catch the first wave of fMRI research, which has since expanded massively into a global science ecosystem. I thought it could only be a matter of time, perhaps a few years, certainly by the time I was 50, before the irresistible flood of new discoveries from brain scanning, and brain science generally, must force radical improvements in how we think about and treat mental health disorders.

It was in that spirit that I started as a Professor of Psychiatry in the University of Cambridge in 1999. At first, I carried on with my brain imaging research, trying to find new ways of measuring and analysing the complex network organisation of the human brain. I am probably most well-known as an academic scientist for my work on network neuroscience or "the connectome". But that is not the topic of this book.

As I approached my mid-40s, I couldn't help noticing that, despite what seemed like a tremendous amount of progress in neuroscience internationally, there was no sign yet of any great change in what was happening day-to-day in local NHS clinics and hospitals. I became restless about the prospect of making any difference to psychiatric practice simply by writing more papers about brain scans. I recognised that the most powerful lever of change in the history of medicine was always the advent of a new treatment. I found myself wanting to know more about how new drug treatments were being discovered for depression, psychosis and other disorders.

That's why, in 2005, I took an unusual chance to start working half-time for GlaxoSmithKline, also known as GSK, one of the UK's biggest pharmaceutical companies. Half the week I spent working in my University lab on the fascinating esoterica of network analysis and the other half I spent working as the director of GSK's clinical research unit, conveniently located about 200 yards down the hall in Addenbrooke's Hospital. In the GSK unit, we did a lot of studies to test the effects of new drugs that were in clinical development for psychiatry, neurology and other areas of medicine. It felt exhilarating at times to be inching closer to the promise of new treatments; but then, in 2010, GSK abruptly closed down all its research and development programs in mental health. I realised I was a 50-year-old psychiatrist working for a company that didn't want to do psychiatry any more. And if a company as big and strong as GSK didn't see an opportunity to make therapeutic progress in psychiatry, what did that mean for the prospects of those radical improvements in treatment that I had been confidently expecting to witness for the last 20 years? That is the moment I began to start thinking seriously about the ideas that this book is about.

I became increasingly interested in the work of other scientists who had been pioneering a new field of research that linked the brain and the mind to the workings of the immune system. They called it immuno-psychiatry or neuro-immunology. The first time I heard of it, to be honest, it sounded bonkers to me, for all sorts of good reasons. But as I delved into it deeper, it seemed increasingly plausible that this might be a scientific strategy that was different enough to offer a fresh chance of making therapeutic progress in psychiatry. I talked to lots of people and once again I was lucky. My GSK boss agreed it could be worth looking into and from about 2013 we were supported by the Medical Research Council and the Wellcome Trust to set up research partnerships with other companies and academic experts to find out more about the links between inflammation and depression.

Hopefully that explains how I came to be involved in the immuno-psychiatry research program that I am still working on scientifically; but it doesn't explain why I wrote a book about it. Scientists are highly incentivised to write papers for a technically specialised readership of their professional colleagues, rather than books that almost anyone might read. But as I have spent the last five years or so learning more about how the immune system and the nervous system interact, how inflammation of the body can cause mental symptoms like depression, it has increasingly seemed to me that these questions resonate widely. They touch on some very basic ideas about the relationship between the body and the mind, as well as the traditional difference between psychiatry and the rest of medicine. And they point towards not just a few new anti-depressant drugs but a radically reconfigured –

dare I say, radically better – way of dealing with mental and physical health disorders together, rather than apart, as we currently do.

This book does contain some technical language, especially in relation to the immune system, because if I tried to tell the story without any technical details I would not be telling it like it really is. And it is, I think, a really exciting story of how we could begin to see new science make a surprising difference to mental health. I hope you enjoy it.

Ed Bullmore
Cambridge, UK
March 2018

Chapter 1

DARING TO THINK DIFFERENTLY

We all know depression. It touches every family on the planet. Yet we understand surprisingly little about it.

This dawned on me in an acutely embarrassing way one day in my first few years of training as a psychiatrist, when I was interviewing a man in the outpatient clinic at the Maudsley Hospital in London. In response to my textbook-drilled questioning, he told me that his mood was low, he wasn't finding any pleasure in life, he was waking up in the small hours and unable to get back to sleep, he wasn't eating well and had lost a bit of weight, he was guilty about the past and pessimistic about the future. "I think you're depressed," I told him. "I already know that," the patient told me, patiently. "That's why I asked my GP to refer me to this clinic. What I want to know is why am I depressed and what can you do about it?"

I tried to explain about anti-depressant drugs, like selective serotonin reuptake inhibitors, or SSRIs, and how they worked. I found myself burbling about serotonin and the idea that depression was caused by a lack of it. Imbalance was the word I had heard more experienced psychiatrists deploy with aplomb on these occasions. "Your symptoms are probably caused by an imbalance of serotonin in your brain and the SSRIs will restore the balance to normal," I said, waving my hands around to show how an imbalanced thing could be rebalanced, how his wonky mood would be restored to equilibrium. "How do you know that?" he asked. I started to repeat all the stuff I had just learnt from the textbooks about the serotonin theory of depression, before he interrupted: "No, I mean how do you know that about me? How do you know that the level of serotonin is imbalanced in my brain?" The truth is that I didn't.

That was about 25 years ago, and we still don't have confident or consistent answers to these and many other questions about where depression comes from or what to do about it. Is depression all in the mind? Is my depression "just" the way I am thinking about things? But then why is it so often treated with drugs that work on nerve cells? Is it "really" all in the brain? To our friends and family who are depressed, we may not know what to say. If we are depressed ourselves, we may feel ashamed to say so.

The silence around depression and other mental health disorders is less deafening now than it was. We are getting better at talking about it, which is good, even if we don't always agree with each other. We can see that depression is very common, it can be really disabling in many ways and it can reduce both the quality of life – depressed people have less experience of pleasure – and the quantity of life – depressed people have reduced life expectancy. We're not surprised to read that the economic costs of depression and related disorders are so vast[1, 2] that if we could completely cure depression in the UK from the start of the next financial year it would be roughly equivalent to adding 4% to GDP, or tripling the projected annual growth rate of the whole economy from 2% to 6%. If the country somehow became totally un-depressed, we'd boost our national wealth massively.

But despite our growing awareness of how commonly depressive episodes and disorders crop up among people we know, and the massive scale of the public health challenge that depression represents globally, we still have only limited ways of dealing with it. There are some widely available and moderately effective treatments out there; but there have been no breakthrough advances in the last 30 years. What we had for depression in 1990 – serotonin-tweaking drugs, like Prozac, and psychotherapy – is pretty much still all that we've got therapeutically. And that's evidently not good enough: otherwise depression wouldn't be on track to become the biggest single cause of disability in the world by 2030.

We must dare to think differently.

One day in 1989, when I was training as a physician, just before I started to specialise in psychiatry, I saw a woman in her late fifties with an inflammatory disease called rheumatoid arthritis. I'll call her Mrs P. She had been arthritic for many years. The joints in her hands were painfully swollen and disfigured by scarring. The collagen and bone in her knees had been destroyed so that the joints no longer worked smoothly and she found it difficult to walk. Together we talked through the long list of physical signs and symptoms that are diagnostic of rheumatoid arthritis. She ticked all the boxes. Then I asked her a few questions that weren't on the standard checklist. I asked about her state of mind, her mood, and over the course of the next 10 minutes or so she quietly but clearly told me that she had very low levels of energy, nothing gave her pleasure any more, her sleep was disturbed and she was preoccupied by pessimistic and guilty thoughts. She was depressed.

I was pleased with myself. I thought I had made a minor medical discovery by doubling her diagnoses. She had come to see me with rheumatoid arthritis; I had added depressive disorder. I rushed to tell my senior physician this important news: "Mrs P is not only arthritic, she's also depressed." He was not impressed by my diagnostic acumen. "Depressed? Well, you would be, wouldn't you?"

We could both recognise that Mrs P was depressed and she was inflamed. However, the conventional medical wisdom of the time was that she was depressed because she knew she had a chronic inflammatory disease. It was all in the mind. It did not occur to either of us that it might originate in the body. That Mrs P might be depressed – not because she knew she was inflamed – but simply because she *was* inflamed. Mrs P left the clinic no less likely to be depressed or fatigued than she was when she'd arrived. We'd not dared to think differently and we'd done nothing to make a difference.

About 30 years down the road, we are becoming much more fluent in a new way of thinking scientifically about the links between depression and inflammation, between mind and body, as I recently discovered for myself after a visit to the dentist.

Root canal blues

A few years ago I had an old filling in one of my molars that had gone rotten, become infected, and my dentist needed to drill out the cavity all the way to the tips of the roots of the tooth. Undergoing root canal surgery is not my favourite way to while away an hour or so but I knew it had to be done. I was cheerful enough when I obediently hopped up on the chair and opened wide. But as soon as it was all done, I wanted to go home, to go to bed and not talk to anyone. And when I was alone at home I found myself cogitating gloomily on the grave until I went to sleep.

The next morning I got up, went to work and forgot about mortality. I had endured some drilling of my tooth, some bruising of my gums, and I had briefly experienced some mental and behavioural symptoms: lethargy, social withdrawal, morbid rumination. You could say I had been a bit depressed: but – hey – who likes going to the dentist?

There seems to be nothing out of the ordinary about this sequence of events – and there isn't – but the ordinary explanation for it turns out to be not the only one.

The traditional way of thinking about this tiny episode of illness starts with my body's immune response to infection and injury. My tooth had been infected by some bacteria; my gums had become inflamed in response to that infection; the dentist's drilling and scraping, although intended to achieve a long-term surgical cure, had the short-term disadvantage of making my gums even more inflamed and increasing the risk of the bacteria spreading from my tooth into my bloodstream. The reason I went to the dentist, and what happened to me when I got there, amounted to a challenge to my body's integrity, a threat to my survival and a clarion call to my immune system to step up its inflammatory response.

Working out this mechanistic chain of cause and effect, which leads from a physical attack, like an injury or an infection, to an inflammatory response from the immune system, is one of the truly game-changing triumphs of scientific medicine. This is the triumph of immunology, the science that now permeates our understanding of almost all diseases, and underpins the therapeutic success of vaccination, transplant surgery and successful new drugs for diseases like rheumatoid arthritis, multiple sclerosis and increasingly more kinds of cancer. This immensely powerful science can provide a minutely detailed explanation for how infection in my tooth could cause local inflammation of my gums, and how surgery could exacerbate the inflammation acutely.

But immunology has not yet had nearly so much to say about what inflammation feels like for the inflamed patient, or how inflammation can have effects on thoughts and behaviour. Why did I want to be by myself? Why did I want to go to bed and stay there? Why was I so gloomy? The answers to questions like these have traditionally come from psychology, rather than immunology.

Thus I told myself a psychological story, that my close encounter with the dentist must have reminded me that I was literally getting long in the tooth. And this concrete affirmation of a well-worn metaphor for mortality must have triggered a period of rational pessimism as I calculated how much longer I might have to live. To paraphrase my self-diagnosis, to put it another way: I became momentarily depressed because I *thought about* the implications of my root canal surgery. My mental state was a reflection or meditation on my physical state, rather than directly caused by my physical state.

To the extent that you are still unsurprised by this story, you are a dualist. Because the conventional medical explanation for what happened to me is dualist – it exists in two domains – physical and mental – with only a nebulous point of connection between them. Everything that happened up to and including my visit to the dentist is precisely explained in the physical domain, by the biological science of infection and immunity. Everything that happened to my mood and behaviour after I went to the dentist is explained in the mental domain, by the psychologically meaningful story I told myself about getting long in the tooth.

At the time, about 2013, when I explained my own experience of inflammation and depression in this way, I found it somewhat comforting "to know". Now, looking back, I am finally surprised. I am surprised to realise how incomplete and convoluted the standard dualist explanation seems to be – now that I know there could be a very different kind of explanation for what happened to me. There is another way of thinking about my root canal blues. I could have been momentarily depressed simply because I was inflamed; not because I thought about the consequences of being inflamed. The brief, transient burst of inflammation in my mouth could directly have caused the changes in my mood, behaviour and cognition that I noticed immediately after the surgery.

This new explanation is logically simpler than the familiar dualist reasoning I used when I told myself the story about getting long in the tooth. The stream of explanatory narrative doesn't run into the sand in the physical domain, when I get out of the dentist's chair, and then miraculously resurface in the mental domain, when I am back at home despondently in bed. Now the chain of cause and effect can run from start to finish in the physical domain – from the initial cause of an infected tooth to the final effect of a depressed mood.

But causality is tough to nail down, scientifically. To be completely confident that inflammation can cause depression we'd want to know the answers to two big questions:

How, exactly, step by step, can inflammatory changes in the body's immune system cause changes in the way the brain works so as to make people feel depressed?

Why is a depressed patient inflamed in the first place? And why should the body's inflammatory response, which is supposed to be on our side, which has evolved to help us win the battle against disease, be causing us to feel depressed?

Back when I met Mrs P, about 30 years ago, these questions about causality were almost unasked and there were no good scientific or medical answers to them.

By the time of my root canal surgery in 2013, the questions were being asked much more often, and more precisely, and the answers were becoming clearer, thanks to the work of a disruptive new science, which has continued to make rapid progress in the last 5 years.[3-6]

Like a lot of new science, this one has emerged at the interfaces between more established domains of knowledge. It exists at the boundaries between immunology, neuroscience, psychology and psychiatry. It goes by a variety of ungainly, often hyphenated names – like neuro-immunology or immuno-psychiatry – that speak to its hybrid origins and its transgressive ambitions to link brain, body and mind by the mechanisms of the immune system. Neuro-immunology investigates how the immune system interacts with the brain or nervous system; whereas immuno-psychiatry is more focused on how the immune system interacts with the mind and mental health.

Neuro-immunology and immuno-psychiatry

The first few people brave enough to call themselves neuro-immunologists were a tiny tribe regarded with some condescension and suspicion by more mainstream scientists. It wasn't considered professionally respectable to investigate connections between the brain – the province of neuroscience – and the immune system – the province of immunology. Not respectable not least because it was well known in the 20th century that the brain and the immune system had nothing to do with each other. The white blood cells and antibodies of the immune system circulated in the bloodstream and could pass through the spleen and lymph nodes and various other immunologically important organs of the body. But the cells and proteins of the body's immune system couldn't percolate so freely through the brain because it was protected by something called the blood-brain barrier. The BBB, as it's also known, was explained to me at medical school in the 1980s as something like a Berlin wall that kept the immune system completely apart from the nervous system. The solidity of the BBB exposed the nascent theories of neuro-immunology to the withering scorn of more traditionally minded scientists. How could neuro-immunologists seriously propose – as they began to do from about 1990 – that levels of inflammatory proteins measured by a blood test had anything to do with the brain or the mind, when it was well known that proteins couldn't cross the barrier between blood and brain? It wasn't just wrong; it was worse than that.

The Berlin wall concept of the BBB was the physical embodiment of powerful older ideas, the dualist ideas dating back to Descartes, that mind and body, as we now say, or soul and body, as he said, are utterly different. The 17th-century philosophy of Cartesian dualism is the foundational bedrock of Western scientific medicine. And the disembodiment of the brain by the rigid interdiction of the BBB was a concrete realisation of this philosophy. So when the pioneer neuro-immunologists proposed that inflammatory proteins in the blood could get across the BBB to have effects on the mind, they weren't regarded merely as wrong about the biology but as deeply disrespectful of the philosophical underpinnings of scientific medicine.

It is now clear that a lot of what I was taught in medical school is wrong. It has become increasingly obvious that the existence of the BBB does not prohibit all immunological cross-talk between the brain and the body. We now know that inflammatory proteins in the blood, called cytokines, can send signals across the BBB, from the body to the brain and the mind. I will say more about cytokines later but if you've never heard of them before you can think of them as hormones which circulate in the bloodstream creating powerful inflammatory effects throughout the body, including the brain. So when the dentist started probing my gums and scraping my teeth, she would have caused immune cells in my mouth to produce cytokines, which then circulated throughout my body in my blood and communicated inflammatory signals across the supposedly impermeable BBB to reach the nerve cells in my brain and cause my mind to become inflamed.

What does an inflamed mind look like?

Mental inflammation, I used to think, without thinking about it too hard, might be similar to physical inflammation. As we have known since Roman times, the body becomes red and swollen when it is inflamed. So I used to imagine the inflamed mind was metaphorically red and swollen, angry and excessive, passionate, out of control and potentially dangerous, closest in psychiatric parlance to a state of mania. But the image of an inflamed mind that I conjure up now is almost the opposite: not a choleric and threatening person but a melancholic and withdrawn one. Like Mrs P, her hands swollen and deformed by inflammatory joint disease, silently wondering why she felt so gloomy and tired. I now think of her as typical of an inflamed mind, not metaphorically speaking, but mechanistically speaking.

The shift from metaphors to mechanisms of the inflamed mind begins by acknowledging the overwhelming evidence for a strong association between inflammation and depression. Simply recognising this association, which is sometimes hiding in plain sight, is the right place to start. But the crucial questions are about causality. For a new, post-dualist way of thinking to take root it must be scientifically established that inflammation is not merely associated or linked with depression but can directly cause depression.

One way of teasing apart cause and effect is by looking at the sequence of events in time. Causes must come before effects. So if inflammation is a cause of depressive symptoms, we would expect to find evidence that inflammation can occur before depression; and there is some such evidence from recent research. For example, a 2014 study of 15,000 children in Bristol and south-west England found that children who were not depressed, but were slightly inflamed at the age of nine, were significantly more likely to be depressed 10 years later as 18-year-olds.[7] This is one of dozens of human studies, and hundreds of animal studies, that have shown that inflammation can anticipate or precede depression or depressive behaviours.

But precedence alone is not sufficient for inflammation to be taken seriously as a cause of depression. Sceptical scientists and doctors will need to know how, by what exact biological mechanisms, inflammation can cause depression, step by step from cytokines in the blood to changes in the brain that can in turn cause depressive changes in mood. Here too there is supportive evidence from recent experiments in animals and humans.

If a rat is experimentally injected with infectious bacteria, it behaves a bit like I did after the dentist. It withdraws from social contact with other animals, it doesn't move so much, its sleeping and eating cycles are disturbed. In short, infection reliably causes a syndrome in animals – called sickness behaviour – that is roughly recognisable as akin to the human experience of depression. In fact, you don't even need to infect a rat to see this sickness behaviour. It is enough to inject the rat with cytokines, proving that it is not the germ itself that causes sickness behaviour but the immune response to infection. Inflammation directly causes depression-like behaviours in animals – that is beyond doubt.[3]

We also understand how inflammation can have effects on the brains of rats and mice. We know that nerve cells exposed to cytokines are more likely to die and less likely to be regenerated. We know that when nerve cells are inflamed the connections or synapses between them are less capable of learning patterns of information and that inflammation reduces the supply of serotonin as a transmitter between nerve cells. For animals, at least, an explanatory chain is taking shape that can link inflammation of the body directly to changes in how nerve cells work in the brain, that in turn causes sickness behaviour that looks like depression.

To work out the equivalent chain of connections in humans is not easy. We can't experimentally infect people with dangerous bacteria, we can't inject cytokines (or anything else) directly into the brains of healthy people, and it is impossible to see what inflammation does to living human nerve cells, one cell at a time. The vast majority of human nerve cells – about 100 billion of them – are packed together densely in the brain; and the brain is extremely well protected from the outside world by the bony skull. The only way we can "see" what is going on inside the skull of a living human is with brain scanning techniques, like magnetic resonance imaging. And recent fMRI research has begun to produce evidence that inflammation of the body can have a direct causal effect on the human brain and mood. For example, when healthy young people were injected with a vaccine against typhoid, their immune systems reacted like the immune system of a rat injected with bacteria, and cytokine levels spiked in their blood. The vaccinated volunteers also became mildly depressed and their post-vaccination depression was associated with greater activation of regions of the brain that we know are hard-wired for emotional expression.[8]

So the science of immuno-psychiatry has matured to the point that it can help me answer the question of how I became depressed after the dentist in a new and logically seamless way. I don't need a ghost in the machine. I can plausibly argue that the surge of cytokines caused by my root canal surgery sent an inflammatory signal across the BBB to cause a change in the emotion-processing networks of nerve cells in my brain, which in turn caused an episode of depression that led my mind to dwell on the grave. There is credible experimental evidence for every step of this dualism-defying, extraordinary explanation. But still it is not entirely complete. There are gaps and anomalies in the existing evidence base, to be sure, as there always will be in any rapidly advancing area of science. But even if we had a complete answer to the question "how", we would still want to know the answer to the question "why".

The only scientifically acceptable answer to that question is in terms of evolution. Why does inflammation cause depression? It can only be because of natural selection. There must be some sense in which a depressive response to infection or any other inflammatory challenge is (or was) advantageous for our survival.[9, 10] And we must have inherited genes that were naturally selected in previous generations to make us more likely to benefit from a depressive response to inflammation. If I want to, I can reasonably speculate that the reason why I became momentarily depressed after the dentist is because I have inherited genes that helped my ancestors survive infections in the past. This genetic inheritance might well have helped me recover from the minor trauma of root canal treatment by aggressively killing off any infectious germs and by dictating that I should stay in bed and conserve my energy while that happened.

Of course, the real importance of these linked new sciences of neuro-immunology and immuno-psychiatry is not that they give me a different way of explaining why I don't like going to the dentist. What matters much more is that once we have begun to map a path to follow from the body, via the immune system, to the brain and the mind – once we have articulated a post-dualist concept of the inflamed mind – we should be able to find entirely new ways of dealing with mental health disorders.

The revolution will not be televised

Depression, schizophrenia, autism, addiction, Alzheimer's disease... there is a long and mournful list of disorders that psychiatrists, clinical psychologists and neurologists ordinarily treat either as if they were "all in the mind" or as if they were "all in the brain". Let's say I had not bounced back to work the day after the dentist. Let's imagine I had become progressively more withdrawn and melancholic until my wife had eventually persuaded me to see a doctor. What would have happened? My GP would probably have asked me a few questions about my state of mind and then offered a course of psychotherapy (to resolve my issues about mortality) or a prescription of anti-depressants (to correct some notional imbalance of serotonin or other neurotransmitters in my brain). It is unlikely my doctor would have attached much diagnostic significance to the root canal story. It is virtually certain that he would not have ordered a blood test to measure cytokine levels, or to see if I had genetic risk factors for a depressive response to inflammation. It is inconceivable that he would have recommended an anti-inflammatory drug (like aspirin) instead of an anti-depressant (like Prozac). In all probability, I would have been sensibly, competently, traditionally treated as if my mood had nothing to do with my immune system. Just like I had traditionally treated Mrs P.

Scientifically there may still be questions to resolve about causality but the link between inflammation and depression is indisputable. So why am I so confident that the doctor I might have consulted about post-dental depression would pay no attention to my immune system? The answer is partly just that medicine is a conservative, highly regulated profession. It is not unusual for changes in practice to lag several decades behind conceptual advances in biological science. A good example of the sometimes slower-than-hoped-for pace of medical progress is the real-life impact of the double helix.

Watson and Crick published the architectural principles of deoxyribonucleic acid (DNA) in 1953,[11] opening up entirely new fields of genetic science and molecular biology. This was a critical turning point in the formation of what became the central orthodoxy of biology – the theory that genetic information is coded by the sequence of DNA molecules, and that different sequences of DNA specify how different proteins are assembled by precisely stringing together hundreds of thousands of amino acids. Since proteins are an enormously large and diverse group of molecules in the human body – including antibodies, cytokines, enzymes and many hormones – our deeper understanding of how protein synthesis is genetically controlled by DNA has been widely recognised as one of the most important advances in the history of biology.

About 50 years later, when President Bill Clinton celebrated the sequencing of the human genome at a White House ceremony in January 2000, he spoke with unbounded millennial optimism about the genome: "without a doubt the most important, most wondrous map ever produced by humankind".[12] He saw this as a scientific advance with the potential to deliver medical breakthroughs on an extraordinary scale and at an extraordinary rate. "It is now conceivable that our children's children will know the term cancer only as a constellation of stars." Now, almost 20 years after he spoke those words, Bill Clinton is a grandfather but we are nowhere near consigning the word to common use only in horoscopes. In the British National Health Service (NHS) in 2018, genetics has made a life-or-death difference to some patients with leukaemia or breast cancer, who are lucky enough to have a genetic profile that makes them more likely to respond to new anti-cancer medicines. But it will take many more generations for the therapeutic potential of genetics to play out across the whole spectrum of health services.

So it is reasonable to expect a fairly slow burn for

immuno-psychiatry in practice. In the NHS in 2018, immunology has made no difference whatsoever to any patients with depression, psychosis or Alzheimer's disease. There are no licensed medicines or other treatments for depression that act primarily on the immune system. There are fascinating new insights into how high levels of social stress can increase bodily inflammation. And there is growing evidence that people who have experienced adversity or abuse in childhood are more likely to be inflamed as children and adults.[13–15] It is also increasingly clear that depressed patients who are also inflamed are less likely to respond well to treatment with conventional anti-depressant drugs.[4] But there is as yet no well-known way by which doctors or other mental health practitioners can leverage this new knowledge to help people with depression. And until my GP is in a position to offer an immunological treatment for depression, I wouldn't expect him to spend too much time entertaining a fancy new immunological way of thinking about where depressive symptoms come from.

Personally, I expect this to change. I can imagine a future in which the old dividing lines between mental and physical illness are redrawn, the 400-year-old habit of dualist diagnosis is kicked, and the immune system becomes much more central to how we think about – and treat – psychological and behavioural symptoms like depression. I can easily imagine that there could be some decisive moves in this direction over the next five years or so. The lesson of history is that medical revolutions do not make good reality TV. But there is a current of scientific change running under the surface of day-to-day medical practice which could transform the way we deal with depression and other mental health disorders. And that is the idea behind this book. We can move on from the old polarised view of depression as all in the mind or all in the brain to see it as rooted also in the body; to see depression instead as a response of the whole organism or human self to the challenges of survival in a hostile world.

Chapter 2

THE WORKINGS OF THE

IMMUNE SYSTEM

To get to this new way of thinking about depression, we have to start in an unfamiliar place: the realm of the lymph node, the spleen and the white blood cell. This is the realm of immunology, the science of the immune system that explains the mechanisms and rationale for inflammation. Thanks to immunology, we know that inflammation is what happens when the immune system is aroused to defend us against our enemies.

Dealing with inflammation has always been central to medicine and while I was training as a physician, before I started in psychiatry, I studied clinical immunology quite diligently until about 1990. Then I didn't look at an immunology textbook or paper again until about 2012, when I was truly dazzled by what had happened since I last paid attention.

Twenty-first-century immunology is built on some of the same foundations that I was taught in the 20th century – the bare bones of some of the textbook diagrams are the same – but in every respect the picture is now marvellously more detailed and complex. Several completely new things have been discovered. And several old certainties have been destroyed. This new and still growing immunology is scientifically and therapeutically powerful in many unprecedented ways.[16] In particular, as far as we're concerned, it empowers us to think differently about the links between the immune system, the brain, behaviours and states of mind. Your body's state of inflammation, your immune system's level of threat arousal, can have a direct effect on how you feel, and what you think about. To put it more scientifically, inflammation of the body can cause changes in how the brain works, which in turn cause the changes in mood, cognition and behaviour that we recognise as depression.

Inflammation and infection

To see how this works from the ground up, let's start with the basic building blocks of the human body – its microscopic cells – which occur in millions of different varieties, each specialised for a different function. Nerve cells make up most of the nervous system, white blood cells make up most of the immune system and endothelial cells form the inner lining of the arteries and veins in the cardiovascular system. White blood cells can be further subdivided into more specialised immune cells, like macrophages, lymphocytes and microglial cells. These cells are the A-list actors in the immune system (Fig. 1).

The raw material of all cells is protein and there are billions of different proteins in the human body, each built according to a DNA code that we inherited genetically from our parents. All antibodies and enzymes are proteins, as are cytokines and many hormones, like insulin. Many proteins act as biological signals, which communicate information within a cell or between cells, by recognising and binding to another protein, called a receptor. This biological hierarchy of systems, cells, proteins and, ultimately, DNA constitutes an organism, for example a human, like one of us. Inevitably, the human self will be attacked by non-human organisms, like bacteria, collectively called antigens or non-self. Inflammation is what the immune system does to defend the self from the non-self, to protect us against them.

We have known something about inflammation since the ancients. The first recognisable account is attributed to Celsus, a Roman physician who was once so renowned in medical circles that even 1,500 years after his death the most original and boastful physician in medieval Europe could think of no more exalted trade name for himself than Paracelsus (beyond Celsus).

It was Celsus who originally described inflammation as a syndrome, a cluster of diagnostic symptoms and signs: redness, heat, swelling and pain. He recognised that inflammation often followed injury. So, for example, if a man was stabbed in the hand, the wounded area would become hot, red, swollen and painful (Fig. 2). The hand became acutely inflamed – that much was clear by clinical examination, and the concept of acute inflammation has remained enduringly useful to medicine ever since. What was not so clearly resolved until more modern times were the key mechanistic questions: how and why does the body respond

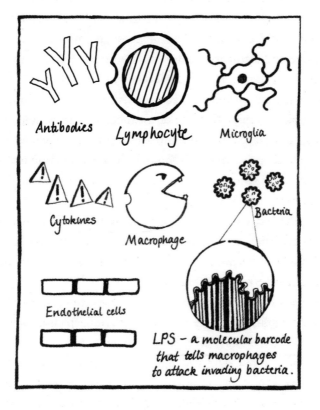

Figure 1: Immune cells. These "immunojis" represent the key players in the immune system. Macrophages are big eating cells that eat bacteria and produce cytokines, or inflammatory hormones. They are ubiquitous in the body. Microglia or microglial cells are macrophages that are located uniquely in the brain. Lymphocytes produce antibodies to help macrophages fight infection. Endothelial cells form the inner lining of arteries and veins.

to injury in this particular way?

Immunology has answered these questions with remarkable precision. We can now see how hundreds of proteins interact with each other in complex signalling pathways to translate the traumatic stimulus of the wound into an inflammatory response. We can spell out step by step a molecular chain of cause and effect that explains how the inflammatory response to injury dilates the local blood vessels, allowing more blood to flow into the wounded area, causing the ancient symptom of heat. We know exactly how inflammation makes blood vessel walls leakier, allowing more fluid to leave the circulation and accumulate in the muscles and other tissues of the hand, causing the classical symptom of swelling. We know these and many other biological details about how the immune system generates an inflammatory response. We now also know why.

Inflammation and immunity are what keep us alive in a hostile world. We know that people who are unfortunate enough to be born without a fully functioning immune system, due to a rare genetic mutation, often do not survive

Figure 2: Inflammation. (Clockwise from top) From the time of the earliest humans, fighting and conflict have been a common cause of physical injury and infection. In modern times, immunology has explained how the body makes an inflammatory response to the trauma and invasion by hostile bacteria caused by a knife wound. Macrophages eat the bacteria contaminating the knife blade and release cytokines into the bloodstream, which attract more macrophages to swarm into the wounded area to overwhelm the bacteria and successfully defend the self from the non-self. These microscopic workings of the immune system explain the classical symptoms and signs of acute inflammation – swelling, redness and tenderness of the wounded hand.

very long after birth. Without an immune system, we are easy meat for our enemies. And we are surrounded by enemies that ancient physicians like Celsus simply couldn't see: bugs, germs, pathogens, viruses, bacteria, worms, protozoa and fungi. There is a very long list of mostly microscopic organisms that have evolved to succeed by infecting us. And generally their success is our failure.

If the knife that stabs the hand is dirty, or even if it is ordinarily clean rather than rigorously disinfected, the blade will be covered with bacteria. The stabbed hand will be infected by whatever bacteria are contaminating the knife and once the bacteria are comfortably at home in the hand they will start to proliferate, to reproduce at an astonishing rate. What will this do to us? It depends partly on what types or species of bacteria happened to be sitting on the knife in the first place. There are millions of different bacterial species in the world and they are not all equally dangerous to humans.

But let's suppose that one of the bacteria contaminating the knife was *Clostridium tetani*. That could turn a minor injury into a cause of death; because *C tetani* – as you might have guessed – causes tetanus. More mechanistically speaking, it produces a poison or toxin that gets into the nervous system and upsets the normal balance between excitation and inhibition of nerve cells. The poisoned nerve cells become uninhibitedly excited and send non-stop signals to the muscles, causing them to contract in prolonged and painful spasms. The first sign is typically lockjaw. The muscles that normally open and close the mouth become permanently contracted so that the mouth can no longer open: the patient can no longer speak, eat or drink. Likewise tetanic spasm of the facial muscles causes the corners of the mouth to be uplifted so that, even as the patient is suffering severely, becoming progressively, painfully paralysed to the point of immobility and death, he wears a fixed expression of mild amusement, a sardonic smile.

So that's what we're up against and always have been up against. We are constantly under attack by hostile and dangerous enemies. It is our immune system that defends each of us – the self – from the biological warfare waged against us by alien organisms – the non-self. And there are key features of the immune system's organisation that equip it superbly for this vital defensive role: its location, its methods of communication and its capacity for rapid rebuttal and learning.

But, marvellous though it is, the immune system is not infallible. It can make mistakes. And when the immune system gets it wrong it can become a cause of diseases as serious as the diseases it defends us against so brilliantly when it gets it right. We'll start with the upside.

Location, location, location

This doesn't just mean that location is very important for the immune system; but also that the immune system is in many locations. Most of the nervous system is compactly located in the head. Most of the respiratory system is encaged in the chest. The immune system is not like that. You can't point to one place in your body and say "that's where my immune system is". The immune system is nowhere because it is everywhere.

It has to be everywhere because infectious attack can come from anywhere. Viruses and bacteria can infect the body through multiple different portals – some can penetrate the skin, others are infectious through the lungs or the gut. Any surface between the self and the non-self, between the body and the outside world, is open to attack; and all such surfaces are frontlines of biological warfare between hostile non-self agents – like *C tetani* – and the perimeter defences of the self.

The immune cells that are most widely distributed throughout the body and that guard most of the perimeter are called macrophages. This is a 19th-century word made up of two ancient Greek roots: macro meaning big and phage meaning eat. You can think of a macrophage – usually pronounced to rhyme with page – as a big cell that eats a lot (Figs. 1 and 2). And what it eats are often bacteria. It destroys hostile germs by enveloping them in a membrane and enzymatically digesting them. It is an extremely effective killing machine but its most powerful weapons against infection are also short-range weapons. To eat the germ, the macrophage obviously has to be in direct physical contact with it. So a single macrophage will only be able to deal immediately with a bacterial infection within a restricted radius – a few millimetres – of its location. To protect the entire perimeter many millions of macrophages have to be stationed like border guards or centurions, each guarding a local patch of tissue, strategically concentrated in positions that are most likely to be attacked.

The gut is a major battleground against infection. The

lining of the gut has to be relatively thin and receptive to the outside world, in order to absorb nutrients from food. It can't be physically protected from infection like the skin, by a tough external layer of keratin, and yet it is continually exposed to the thick broth of bacteria and more-or-less digested food that passes through our bowels on a daily basis. The gut wall is constantly being penetrated by bacteria; and it is constantly being defended by a legion of macrophages that are permanently and densely stationed from mouth to anus.

It is a similar story for the lungs, the genital and urinary tracts, the surface of the eye: anywhere that the body is directly exposed to the outside world, macrophages will be found in abundance, waiting for the first sign of trouble. But however effective the frontline defences, some bacteria will inevitably break through from time to time. They will manage to avoid being eaten immediately, they will proliferate and they will disperse through the flow of blood and lymph around the body. To provide additional defence of key internal organs macrophages are also stationed in the spleen, the liver, the brain, the kidneys, the muscles, the fatty adipose tissue and the bones. The key thing is that the immune system, at least in the form of macrophages, is everywhere (Fig. 3).

Communication: the medium is the message

The next key ingredient of the immune system's defensive game plan is communication. To function as a single, integrated, adaptive system the individual macrophage cells must be coordinated. It is the difference between hundreds of isolated centurions and a Roman legion. The science of how immune cells communicate with each other has been at the heart of the recent explosive growth in immunology.

We now know that there are two main ways that macrophages can communicate with the rest of the immune system: by direct contact with one other cell; or by secretion of cytokines, proteins that can move freely through the body and send a signal to many cells. The cell-to-cell contact mechanism is most useful for communicating very specific information about a particular hostile agent. The cytokine secretion mechanism is better suited for broadcasting a more general message about the current status of an infection or the inflammatory response to it.

Cytokines are secreted from macrophages into the bloodstream, circulate throughout the body like inflammatory hormones, and then bind to specific receptors on the surface of other macrophages, to send them a signal, to make them angrier or more inflamed. For most of its life – and it can live for decades – a macrophage will be sitting quietly on its own, guarding the same small patch of tissue in the gut or the skin, waiting for something to happen. Then suddenly something does happen. The neighbourhood is invaded by a hostile force of rapidly proliferating and potentially overwhelming bacteria. The macrophage needs to warn the rest of the immune system without immediately deserting its position on the front line. It calls for help by pumping out powerful cytokine signals that can diffuse rapidly into the bloodstream, broadcasting a message of alarm, a call to arms, to any other immune cell in the body that can pick up the signal through cytokine receptors on its surface.

Macrophages are highly sensitive to the cytokine signals sent by other macrophages when they need help. These inflammatory cytokines arouse quiescent macrophages, which leave their usual niches and move towards the source of the inflammatory signal, to support their comrade.

For an example of cell-to-cell communication, let's think back to the stabbed hand, and suppose that the wound is infected, which triggers a local inflammatory response, so the hand becomes red and swollen. Then, a few days later, there will also be some swelling in the armpit on the same side as the inflamed hand. You might have experienced something similar when a bad sore throat (local inflammation of the pharynx) was followed a few days later by swelling in your neck. In common parlance, your "glands are swollen"; in medical parlance, there is enlargement of the lymph nodes. In the case of the stabbed hand it is the axillary nodes in the armpit; in the case of the sore throat it is the cervical nodes in the neck.

The reason this happens is that lymph nodes or lymph glands provide a focal point or hub for immune cells to get together and exchange information by direct contact. The axillary lymph nodes become swollen after an infection in the hand because many of the macrophages that have successfully engaged with the bacterial enemy then travel away from the frontline to the nearest lymph node (which happens to be in the armpit if you start from the hand or in the neck if you start from the pharynx). These macrophages that are pouring into their neighbourhood lymph nodes are not running away from a fight; they are reporting back to the immune system as a whole. They are communicating vital,

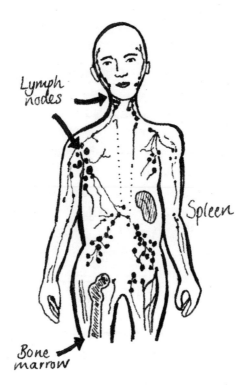

Figure 3: The immune system. We can look at the immune system anatomically: where is it? Lymph nodes in the armpits and elsewhere are connected to each other by a branching network of lymphatic vessels, which allows immune cells to circulate freely throughout the body and to enter the bloodstream. Immune cells in the blood are called white blood cells. The spleen stores immune cells and the bone marrow is important for making new immune cells.

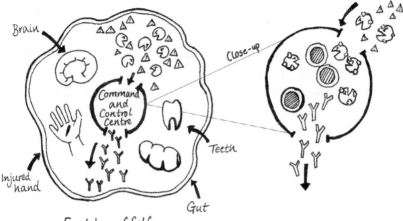

Brain

Close-up

Command
and
Control
Centre

Teeth

Injured
hand

Gut

Front line of Self

Or we can look at the immune system physiologically: what is it doing?
The immune system is helping us to survive, defending the self against
ceaseless attack on all fronts. The macrophages are the front-line troops,
trained by evolution to attack hostile bacteria on sight, to eat them, and
to carry digested fragments of eaten bacteria on their surface as a way
of telling the lymphocytes, the generals of the immunoji army, exactly
what a piece of the enemy looks like. Macrophages communicate with
lymphocytes in lymph nodes, spleen, bone marrow and the other
command-and-control centres of the immune system. Lymphocytes
can pump antibodies into the circulation to help macrophages defend
the self against attack immediately and in the future.

detailed intelligence about the nature of the enemy. Each of them is carrying small protein fragments of the bacteria they have eaten and digested, pieces of the non-self invader, also known generally as antigens. Different macrophages carry randomly different fragments, randomly different antigens, and they crowd into lymph nodes each in search of another immune cell – a lymphocyte – that will recognise their piece of the antigenic puzzle and know what to do about it. The macrophages swirl through the lymph nodes, speed-dating, making brief contact with one lymphocyte after another, until they literally bump into one, maybe the one and only, lymphocyte in that node that can read the signal about the enemy they are bringing back to HQ from the front line. If the macrophage is like a centurion then a lymphocyte is more like a general. Or if you prefer to think of the macrophage as a robotic enforcer or robocop then the lymphocyte is more like an intelligence agent or spook.

Once the macrophage has found the right lymphocyte to report to, the couple will stay locked together for several days, in a briefing conference about the detailed content of the anti-genic message, before the lymphocyte decides to take action, often to escalate or diversify the immune response initially triggered by the macrophages (Fig. 3).

Direct contact between immune cells is crucial for commu-nication in detail about the antigen – the nature of the enemy. It is also time consuming (it takes days for the lymph nodes to swell after infection), hit and miss (most contacts between cells do not lead to communication), and it requires special venues. Cells meet each other mainly in lymph nodes, which are clustered in the armpits, the groin, the neck and all along the midline of the thoracic and abdominal cavities. Cells meet each other in patches of lymphoid tissue like the tonsils and the adenoids, which are located throughout the gut. And cells meet each other in the spleen, the bone marrow and the thymus gland. These are sometimes called the organs of the immune system (Fig. 3). We can think of them all as command-and-control centres, places where immune cells congregate to talk to each other face to face about the current state of threat on the front line and how to respond to it.

Rapid rebuttal and learning

The immune system has an innate capacity to detect and respond with extreme prejudice to whatever it recognises as non-self and therefore potentially dangerous. This rapid rebuttal function depends especially on the front-line army of macrophages, which has been trained by evolution to respond very fast and very forcefully to the first signs of infection.

Speed of response is important because bacteria and viruses – the enemy – can reproduce so fast. A single germ of *C tetani* can become two in about 20 minutes and that number will keep doubling every 20 minutes. By the scary logic of exponential growth, one bacterium can become millions of bacteria within a few hours. The immune system needs to win the battle quickly – or at least put a dent in the enemy – before the balance of forces tips decisively in favour of the invaders.

So each macrophage on the front line needs to be able to

make a snap decision: self or non-self, friend or foe? It needs to make that decision autonomously, without any time-consuming consultation with other cells. But how can it be expected to respond so quickly and decisively to an unpredictable and perhaps unprecedented threat? There are millions of different types of bacteria and viruses out there in the hostile world and no single macrophage can have met them all before. But all macrophages have inherited the wisdom of their ancestors. Each of them is innately prepared to recognise at first sight an enemy it has never seen before.

The biological war between humans and germs has been raging continuously since *Homo sapiens* first evolved as a distinct species more than 150,000 years ago. The war between mammals and bacteria, or between multi-cellular organisms and single-cell invaders, has been ongoing for aeons. And throughout the entire stretch of biological history, the first commandment of evolution has been obeyed: only the fittest shalt survive. The ancestors that survived to breed and pass on their genes to subsequent generations will often have survived infection. Genetic mutations that conferred even the slightest advantage to resist infection will have been naturally selected. So that by a long and winding road of random genetic mutation and ruthless natural selection, your macrophages have been trained to detect and respond to threats that you personally may never before have encountered, in your lifetime of decades, but that your ancestors will have encountered and survived in an evolutionary lineage dating back to the dawn of biological time.

For example, you may never have visited Africa in your life. Then one year you go there on holiday and your immune system, especially the immune system in your gut, is suddenly exposed to swarms of exotic, unfamiliar bacteria. Since this biological threat is massive and very foreign to you, it could be lethal. But over evolutionary time, your immune system has learnt something very useful about bacteria. You might say that your macrophages have been robotically pre-programmed by natural selection. They have been pre-loaded with sophisticated software for on-sight detection and killing of many different bacteria.

The macrophage knows that most of the bacteria that infect the gut, whether in Africa or in America, have something in common. They have a similar biochemical constitution. They have a tough outer wall, to protect them from gut digestion, which is composed of a molecule called lipopolysaccharide, or LPS for short. Crucially, LPS is not a molecule that we make in our bodies, or that our mammalian ancestors made. It is only made by bacteria. Therefore it is a very reliable and convenient guide to the molecular difference between friend and foe. If a cell has LPS molecules on its outer surface then the macrophage doesn't need to know anything else about it – that molecular barcode or pattern alone is enough to signify that it is not one of our own cells, it must be an enemy cell and it must be destroyed. I know this because I have read about it in immunology textbooks. The macrophages in your gut "know this" by natural selection.

The enemy identification and elimination process happens very fast: it is an algorithmic response to automatic pattern recognition – shoot on sight. Every macrophage in your body has been highly trained by evolution, equipped with LPS barcode readers and other devices, to enable an innate immune response. That deep ancestral knowledge – expressed in the genetics and molecular machinery of the macrophage – is what protects us, makes us less naïve than we might have thought, when we travel for the first time to Africa.

The immune system is not only born with knowledge about the enemy it is also smart enough to acquire new knowledge or to learn about the enemy in its lifetime. The most familiar example of immune learning is probably vaccination. Suppose that before going to Africa on holiday, because I know that there is an increased risk of tetanus in tropical countries, I decide to get a tetanus vaccination. This means that I volunteer to be injected with a weakened form of the germ that could kill me if I encountered it for the first time in the wild. What happens next from an immunological perspective?

In the first few hours or days after the vaccination, there will probably be some pain and swelling at the injection site. These classical signs of inflammation indicate an innate immune response by local macrophages to the deliberate injection of potently antigenic, provocatively non-self bacteria. But that is a side effect of the vaccination, not its primary purpose. The point of a vaccination is to stimulate the lymphocytes of the immune system to produce antibodies, proteins that are designed specifically to recognise the antigen and to bind to it. And since these antibodies have been selected for mass production because they specifically recognise the tetanus antigen, and since antibody production tends to keep going for several years once it has started, my immune system will now be doubly prepared for the next time it meets *C tetani*. In addition to the innate immune defences that trigger the shoot-on-sight response of macrophages, inherited from my evolutionary ancestors, I have now acquired an additional line of defence. My immune system has learnt and remembered something about the world in my own lifetime: it has adapted. My lymphocytes have learnt from my vaccination that *C tetani* is out there, it is a real threat, and they need to remain on guard against it by constantly producing antibodies.

Auto-immunity: the flip side

So far I have made the immune system sound like a formidable defensive force, an utterly reliable ally, that manages its ubiquitous location by clear lines of communication between millions of component cells, and that can coordinate sophisticated programmes of rapid rebuttal and adaptive learning to help us survive in a world full of micro-organisms that are out to get us. That is all true but it is not the whole truth. There is also a dark side to the immune system.

I have used war as a metaphor for inflammation and I might have encouraged you to think that the immune system always wins its inflammatory wars like modern, high-tech armies are sometimes supposed to win military wars: by clean, surgical strikes against targets identified by advanced intelligence. But, in fact, inflammatory wars, like military wars, inevitably cause massive collateral damage to innocent bystanders; and the weapons of the immune system, like guns and missiles, can be pointed in the wrong direction to cause casualties by friendly fire.

Macrophages are following a tight programme to seek

and destroy biological aliens that can be identified on sight by molecular barcodes like LPS. When they engulf the invading bacteria, they spew large quantities of digestive enzymes and bacterial fragments into the surrounding tissue. This macrophage exhaust is toxic to innocent bystanders – like bone or muscle or nerve cells – that happen to be in the vicinity of a bacterial infection but are not protagonists in the immune response to it. As more macrophages are recruited to the site of infection by cytokine signalling, the adverse effects of inflammation on local populations of cells become greater. Intense macrophage warfare is effectively analogous to scorched-earth or carpet-bombing tactics in human warfare. There can be massive collateral damage to non-participants in both kinds of conflict. Macrophages might be able to prevent the infection in the wounded hand from spreading throughout the whole body with lethal effect. But if the infection cannot be completely eliminated, merely contained, and the macrophage army becomes entrenched in its positions for months or years, then the normal, healthy tissues of the wounded hand will be permanently degraded. Muscle, skin and bone will be destroyed, at best replaced by tough, fibrous scars. The macrophage defence could cost the wounded man use of his hand for the sake of saving his life.

Whereas macrophages collaterally damage swathes of innocent bystander cells indiscriminately, the friendly fire of the lymphocytes is more focused on the distinction between self and non-self. The immune system is extremely good at making this distinction correctly. But it doesn't always get it right. Sometimes the antigens picked up by macrophages and ferried to lymphocytes are not bits of bacterial proteins but bits of our proteins, molecular fragments of our own tissues. Sometimes the lymphocytes mistakenly presented with these self proteins, as if they were possible enemy barcodes, may then mistakenly direct a hostile immune response against their own self. Instead of producing antibodies against bacteria and other truly non-self antigens, the lymphocytes can start churning out antibodies against self proteins, so-called auto-antibodies.

The disease-causing effects of auto-antibodies can be as dramatic as the disease-curing or disease-preventing effects of antibodies directed against bacteria and viruses. "Good" antibodies against *C tetani* can protect me from a fatal tetanus infection; but "bad" auto-antibodies against my own body can cause equally life-threatening diseases. Sometimes the cells in the pancreas that produce insulin come under friendly fire from the immune system. They are hit by auto-antibodies and destroyed, leaving all the other cells in the pancreas completely unscathed. There is no visible scarring but there has been potentially fatal self-harm. Without cells to produce insulin, the body loses control over the levels of glucose in the blood, and many other aspects of its normal metabolism, and the patient becomes diabetic. In the old days, before insulin replacement treatment was invented for diabetes, many patients passed quickly into a coma and died as a result of this discrete but devastating attack on the self by its own immune system.

But you may be beginning to wonder what any of this has to do with depression. I have talked a lot about infection and trauma; but said nothing about moods or states of mind. How is all this beautifully detailed knowledge about white blood cells, lymph nodes, macrophages and cytokines related to mental health?

Chapter 3

HIDING IN PLAIN SIGHT

It's depressing being ill

Do you remember Mrs P? The woman with arthritis who was depressed, as you would be, wouldn't you? When I look back on that moment of ordinary medical practice in an NHS outpatient clinic, I am struck by the complexity of the ideas buried deep beneath the assumption: you would be depressed, wouldn't you? (If you were in her shoes.) The words imply, to put it less succinctly, that Mrs P had consciously reflected on her situation. She knew she had rheumatoid arthritis, she knew that it was inexorably getting worse, her body was becoming ever more disabled, it wouldn't be long before she couldn't leave her wheelchair. She could certainly foresee her progressive decline to a dismal end. And knowing this had made her depressed. As anyone would be depressed who knew that they shared her fate.

When I consulted a senior physician about her combination of depression and inflammatory disease, that was his theoretical analysis. And there is some truth in it. He was right that it is depressing to know that you are ill, or that your illness is likely to get worse. But he was not so right in his unspoken assumption that "thinking about it" was the only possible

43

way in which a physical illness could cause depression. What it meant in practice was that Mrs P's depression was not his problem. He was a consultant physician, concerned with the physical aspects of her health. Her depression was a normal psychological reaction to her physical disease, it was not rooted in her body and unrelated to the pathological cause of her swollen joints. It lay beyond his domain of expertise – in the realm of the shrink or the priest. There was nothing he could do.

It's an anecdote, admittedly, but not an exceptional case. Two aspects of Mrs P's experience are shared by many other people with rheumatoid arthritis. First, her mental symptoms are not unusual. About 90% of arthritis patients say that fatigue is their principal problem and about 40% are depressed. A sense of "brain fog", or difficulty in thinking and planning clearly, is also common. Psychological symptoms dominate the lists of "unmet clinical needs" compiled by the big arthritis charities and patient advocacy groups. The combination of depression and rheumatoid arthritis, which I thought was so remarkable about Mrs P, turns out to be commonplace, even if still largely invisible.[17]

The second aspect of her experience that many other arthritis patients might recognise is the apparent indifference of her physician. The specialist doctors, called rheumatologists, who attend to most cases of rheumatoid arthritis, pay most attention to evidence of physical disease – fMRI scans of eroded joints and blood tests. That is what they are trained to do and very good at doing. They are much less attentive to psychological or behavioural symptoms. Rheumatologists often don't ask their patients about their energy levels, feelings or thoughts at all. If patients volunteer information about their lethargic, pleasureless states of mind, their physicians may not know what to do, or even what to say. Because they certainly can't say to the patient what they, like Mrs P's consultant, might be automatically thinking: "Yes, I'd be depressed too, if I was you."

What is going on here? Why is something so common, and so important to patients, so reflexively neglected by doctors? Why is the close link between depression and arthritis hiding in plain sight? I blame Descartes.

The *cogito*, God, and the machine

René Descartes was a 17th-century mathematician and philosopher, not a rheumatologist or an immunologist. Yet his ideas continue to exercise a remarkable degree of influence on modern medicine. Cartesian dualism, his most medically important philosophy, is the idea that there are two kinds of thing in the world; there are two domains of experience. There is an outer, physical world, where objects interact with each other mechanistically, by experimentally verifiable rules. And there is an inner, spiritual world, where subjective ideas and emotions form the content of consciousness or one's sense of one's self. Each one of us is divided in two by dualism. Our bodies belong to the physical, objective, unconscious domain and our minds to the spiritual, subjective, conscious domain.

Descartes reached this conclusion in a curious and original way. He started from radical doubt. He sceptically challenged himself to verify everything he thought he knew about the world. He was deeply mistrustful of sensory information as a reliable source of knowledge because in his dreams his senses were actively misleading. He could see and hear and feel things in his dreams that weren't really there, he realised when he woke up. So he asked himself how he could be sure that the apparently real things that he could see when he thought he was awake, and walking around with his eyes open, were any more real than the things he saw when he was dreaming with his eyes closed. How could he be sure that the world around him wasn't a dream from which he had not yet woken?

Ultimately, Descartes decided, the only certainty that survived such extreme doubt was doubt itself. While he was restlessly, rigorously, sceptically cogitating on what he knew, what he didn't know, what he knew he knew, what he didn't know he didn't know, etc, etc, the one thing that Descartes knew beyond doubt was that he was cogitating. I doubt everything, I don't think anything is real, I think it's all a dream. I can think whatever I like. But however sceptical or dismissive of the world I feel inclined to be, I cannot doubt my doubting self. "I think I am not real" is a contradiction in terms. If I can say that to myself then I know without doubt it cannot be true. Or to put it the other way round, *cogito ergo sum,* I think, therefore I am, must be true.

Those are the most famous words he wrote but Descartes is also often remembered as one of the principal architects of the scientific revolution, one of the founding fathers of modern science, his name uttered in the same breath as those of his close contemporaries Galileo and Newton. Yet it is not immediately obvious how these two aspects of his reputation can be reconciled. How could a man who has reached the solipsistic conclusion that he knows nothing with certainty, except his own thoughts, be the same man who is credited with setting the world on the path to a more certain scientific knowledge of almost everything? The answer, perhaps surprisingly, was God.

Descartes was a devout Catholic writing at a time, just after the Reformation, when religious belief was more culturally mainstream and more intensely debated than it is now. Descartes believed that he was an immortal and materially insubstantial soul and this soul was what animated his thoughts, his doubts and every other species of his consciousness, including his moments of communion with God. Following a medieval line of reasoning, Descartes argued that his cosmic vision of a perfect and infinite God could not have been falsely invented or misinterpreted by him, because God transcended his human, mortal and finite capacities for imagination. A man couldn't simply imagine God if God didn't exist. The fact that men of advanced reason, like Descartes, commonly could conceive of God was proof positive that God existed. His belief in a benevolent God was axiomatic: not only was God real but God had to be real.

And Descartes believed that God would benevolently protect him, and others like him, from error if they used their mental faculties as diligently and critically as possible to make sense of things. It was God that made the rest of the world potentially knowable to Descartes, rescued him from the certain isolation of knowing only *cogito ergo sum* and opened his mind to experimental science.

As Descartes used mathematics to define the abstract

physical mechanisms that controlled the appearance of things, he began to think of the world as a machine. He saw the human body as a machine, built up of many component parts – like nerves, blood vessels and muscles – which interacted with each other according to the same physical laws that governed the mechanisms of animals and inanimate machines. Physics was the trunk of the tree of scientific knowledge, said Descartes, meta-physics (aka God) was the root, and all other sciences were branches off the trunk. This vision of the body as a physical machine, which Descartes was arguably the first person to see and to articulate compellingly, was the prospectus on which the whole extraordinary success of biology and scientific medicine has since been built.

Of course, at the time, Descartes didn't have a clue what was really going on in the human body. Understanding how the body machine was built was the business of anatomy, which in practice meant dissecting human corpses. This had been widely forbidden for religious reasons for at least the previous 2,000 years. The first anatomical drawings of the heart and the brain that look reasonably accurate to a modern eye did not begin to appear until about 100 years before Descartes. Understanding how the body machine actually worked was the business of physiology and this was in an even more primitive state. The 17th-century physician, William Harvey, had just published the first correct theory on the circulation of the blood at about the same time as Descartes was incorrectly assuming that the blood was expelled from the heart by being heated and expanded in some way.

If the first drafts of the Cartesian body machines now seem to be full of errors and absurdities in detail, they still seem remarkably ambitious in scope. Descartes may have known almost nothing about the body machine compared to what we know now, but he was convinced that all would be knowable, and that ultimately all of animal life would be explicable by the physical mechanisms of the body. For animals, it was simple. They did not have a soul, just the machine. For humans, it was not so straightforward. The mechanistic physics of the body could not be allowed to explain everything about a human as this would exclude the meta-physics of the soul. And the soul was a given, for Descartes; it was real and it had to be. So he was forced to the compromise that there must be a body machine, and there must also be a soul, and both must be combined to make a human. But what then did the soul do, that the body couldn't do? Where was the soul located in the body? And how did the soul and the body interact?

His own efforts to answer these questions never satisfied Descartes.[18] High intellectual prowess and divine communion were surely spiritual; but what about emotions and memories – could they be entirely animal, ultimately explicable by the laws of physics? The bodily location of the soul was also difficult to pinpoint anatomically. Descartes considered a number of possible candidates before settling on the pineal gland, a small and otherwise obscure structure that had recently been dissected in the human brain. Descartes liked the look of the pineal gland because it was singular and central, whereas most of the brain is symmetrically organised. There is a pair of cerebral hemispheres, right and left, and most of the component parts of the brain machine are duplicated in both hemispheres. This would not do for the location of the soul because of its unique and indivisible nature. There were a few other singular structures in the brain, like the pituitary gland, which might conceivably provide suitable accommodation for the soul; but Descartes preferred the pineal gland because he thought it was more mobile.

These anatomical factoids shakily supported his mechanistic theory for how the body and the soul could interact (Fig. 4). He imagined that "animal spirits" could percolate from the blood into the pineal gland and that the visual scene detected by the eyes was also projected onto the inner walls of the gland, where it was consciously perceived. So the pineal was a place where the body machine could speak to the soul. Descartes also imagined the movements of the pineal gland could provide a mechanism for the soul to command the body. He thought the pineal gland worked as a kind of valve or tap, ceaselessly active as it controlled behaviour by directing the flow of spirit through the nerves to the muscles of the body.

That position roughly marks the end of his extraordinary 20-year intellectual journey: from doubt, to the *cogito*, through God back to the machinery of the world, and ultimately to the conceptual and anatomical awkwardness of *deus ex machina*, the God in the machine that is supposedly a human being. Descartes was nothing if not sceptical about his own ideas. He knew that dualism raised as many questions as it settled, and he was still working on it, when suddenly he died.

Descartes was a man of independent means, having inherited property and therefore not financially driven to do work he didn't want to do. He preferred to live alone, often changing

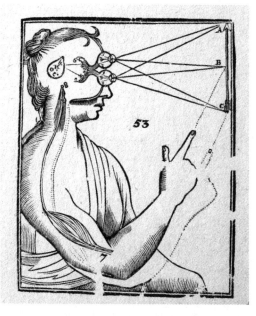

Figure 4: A lady trying to explain the pineal theory of the human mind and body. This is one of the engravings in Descartes' final work, *"Treatise of Man"*,[19] showing how light from an arrow is refracted through the lenses of the eyes to send a visual signal down the optic nerves (coming out of the back of each eyeball), to the pineal gland, drawn as a large droplet or pine seed-shaped thing, marked H, and positioned roughly where you'd expect her right ear to be. The optics and geometry are tip-top. The idea of linking a visual stimulus to a motor response by a physiological circuit is very advanced for the time and remarkably close to the 19th-century concept of a nervous reflex. But the brain anatomy is terrible, even by 17th-century standards. The pineal is drawn in the wrong place and about 10 times bigger than it really is, completely unconnected to the rest of the brain, and connected to the eyes and muscles only by lines of ink on the page. The soul's location has been named but not nailed.

his address to protect his privacy, until, inadvertently, he found himself obliged to deliver philosophy tutorials to the Queen of Sweden three mornings a week from 5 to 10am, a time of day when he naturally preferred to lie in bed, cogitating. One cold and dark February in Stockholm, he developed a chest infection and was dead within 10 days, aged 54. Several years later, his final but inconclusive work was published on the mind/body problem, a problem that didn't so clearly exist before him, a problem that he invented but didn't resolve.

A long shadow

We now know that the details of Cartesian dualism, in its original form, are all wrong. The pineal gland plays a much humbler part in the human body machine than its pivotal, dynamic role in Descartes' scheme. It is a biological clock, sensitive to the daily and seasonal cycles of daylight, and part of the physiological system that maintains a regular, circadian rhythm of alertness and activity every 24 hours. The pineal is important but not of cosmic significance. It doesn't move much, it doesn't control the flow of fluid through the ventricles, it isn't connected to every nerve fibre in the body, it isn't spiritually attuned. If the pineal gland is damaged or lesioned by disease, the patient may complain of a disrupted sleep/wake cycle, but she will not experience disembodied consciousness, a pure state of mind, uninformed or uncontaminated by anything in the physical world.

If Cartesian dualism was an ordinary scientific theory, it

would have been decisively refuted long ago by the mismatch between what Descartes proposed the pineal gland was doing and what it actually does. However, dualism has powerfully endured not so much as a scientific theory but as an idea – one might even say an ideology – about what aspects of human experience are scientifically tractable, and therefore medically respectable.

The Cartesian vision of a human body machine reigns triumphant in medicine. There is universal consensus that the body is made up of atoms and molecules, cells and organs. We can measure it in units like millimetres and seconds. We can expect it to obey universal laws of physics and to be comparable to the biological structures and functions of other animals. All of this makes it scientifically tractable. It may not yet be scientifically understood in every detail but there is no reason to think that it won't become ever more understood in future. And as we have achieved greater scientific understanding of the body, historically, so we have won some therapeutic battles in the fight against disease. We can feel medically in control and progressive about the bodily side of the dualist divide.

But the other side of the human condition – by dualist definition – is something else, embarrassingly different to modern scientific and medical minds. Descartes talked about it unashamedly in spiritual terms; but that was then, 400 years ago, a time when religious idealism still permeated European culture. Descartes also thought he needed God to protect him from experimental error; but the intervening centuries of splendid scientific achievement have made us cockier. We are now confident (with good reason) that we have the logic and the technology safely to do science unchaperoned by God. We have generally reached the view that God has nothing to do with science and science has nothing to tell us about God. So what on earth are we supposed to do about the God in the Cartesian machine?

We can call it the mind or the psyche or consciousness or unconsciousness, instead of the spirit or the soul. We can call it whatever we like. But still it doesn't exist in physical space. It is not clear how it should be measured, if it can be measured at all. We have no reason to expect that it will obey laws of physics, or that other animals have spiritual or mental experiences that are comparable to those of a human mind. And, following the ignominious collapse of the pineal theory, it remains unclear how this mind thing should be related to the body or the brain. All of which makes the mental domain seem scientifically intractable, now and in the future. We do not have the mind under the microscope, we can't see the component parts of its mechanism and therefore we can't expect to be as therapeutically effective in treating diseases of the mind – if it even makes sense to use that expression – as we have become in treating diseases of the body.

However much we admire his scepticism, and celebrate his revolutionary vision of the human body as a machine, Descartes also bequeathed us a conundrum that scientific medicine hasn't yet cracked. In Cartesian medicine the mind and the body aren't the same, they're different kinds of thing, and we still don't know how they are connected to each other. The body is the domain of the physician and know-able by physics and other sciences. The mind is the domain of the psychiatrist or psychologist and knowable only by introspective guesswork, or by inference from behaviour. In Britain in 2018, the NHS is still planned on Cartesian lines. Patients literally go through different doors, attend different hospitals, to consult differently trained doctors, about their dualistically divided bodies and minds.

When I asked Mrs P about her state of mind, in an NHS rheumatology clinic of all places, I unwittingly crossed a philosophical and an organisational line. The senior physician tried to set me straight. Mrs P's depression was not relevant to her joint disease: how could it be? It must be some kind of "mental reaction", some "mortal dread", some reasonable reflection on her progressive disability, the grim reality she faced. She had just been thinking too much about it. Cogitating on the ever-shorter time before she must start using a Zimmer, then a wheelchair. *Cogito ergo sad*, as you might say. Her depression was psychological. And who could blame her? You would be, too, wouldn't you?

Mrs P is not alone

My meeting with Mrs P happened in 1989. Nearly 30 years later it is possible to explain her story in a very different way. This alternative diagnosis is not yet certain knowledge. It's not been baked into the medical training curriculum as a matter of fact. And there are plenty of smart doctors who remain politely sceptical, or frankly incredulous, about what I am going to say next.

Mrs P's depression was directly caused by her inflammatory disease. It was as much a symptom of her rheumatoid disease as her swollen and painful joints. She was depressed because she was inflamed. Once she was depressed, of course, she spent more time sunk in deeply pessimistic and gloomy cogitations about the future, counting the minutes to Zimmer-o' clock. She was cognitively biased by her depression, biased by her inflamed brain to dwell on the worst-case scenario in her future.

Yes, Mrs P knew she was inflamed. She knew she had rheumatoid disease and she knew what that meant. She was a very easy patient to interview, truly an expert by lived experience, who knew how to tell a young doctor she'd never met before exactly what he needed to know about her disease. But I don't believe she was depressed just because she thought about her rheumatoid disease, as a good Cartesian doctor would have it. I accept that it is a depressing shock to know that you have a progressive inflammatory disorder. But I think there are other ways of thinking about Mrs P's predicament. She was depressed not just because she *knew* she was inflamed but, more simply, because she *was* inflamed.

How could that be? How could a joint disease cause depression? Let's start with what is widely agreed about rheumatoid arthritis. Although arthritis means a disease of the joints, rheumatoid is fundamentally a disease of the immune system. The joints in a sense are the victims of an immune disorder, an auto-immune disorder. Rheumatoid disease is caused by the immune system attacking the body – the self – rather than a hostile, infectious enemy – the non-self. The immune system of a rheumatoid patient churns out "bad" auto-antibodies that are designed specifically to bind to the "good" antibodies in the patient's own body. It is as if one part of the immune system thinks the body is under infectious attack by the antibodies produced by another part of the immune system. The immune system starts fighting with itself, pitting "bad" versus "good" antibodies, and then, to make matters worse, the macrophages pile in. The macrophages lurking in the joints and elsewhere in the body jump to the (wrong) conclusion that if there are a lot of auto-antibodies in circulation, if there are a lot of bullets flying through the air, there must be a real enemy in the vicinity. So they start churning out cytokines and spewing out their toxic exhaust, inflaming the joints and carpet-bombing the local neighbourhood. And this can go on for years, because the immune system will not easily be able to eliminate a threat which originates in itself. The lymphocytes will keep on making auto-antibodies and the macrophages will keep on pounding away at a false enemy, damaging muscle and bone and collagen until the patient's joints are chronically disabled. Rheumatoid arthritis is a classic example of the immune system's dark side, its capacity for self-harm.

That's an immunological explanation of how Mrs P's hands became so twisted by scarring that she couldn't take the lid off a jam jar. It doesn't explain why she felt so exhausted when she woke up in the morning that she couldn't get out of bed for breakfast (never mind opening a jam jar). At least it disabuses us of the notion that rheumatoid is a localised disease. It might seem to be localised by clinical examination: some joints are inflamed, others are not. However, the molecular causes of the disease are systemic, not local. Auto-antibodies and cytokines are in circulation throughout the body, not solely concentrated in a few local hotspots. That is why doctors can check the diagnosis of rheumatoid disease by a blood test – cytokines and other inflammatory proteins are increased to concentrations much higher than normal in the blood of a patient like Mrs P. Her whole body was inflamed, not just her joints. And the whole body includes the brain.

Back in 1989, when I agreed with her consultant that Mrs P was rationally depressed as a result of cogitating on her grim prospects, I don't remember asking: "But what if…?" I conceded immediately to the unspoken Cartesian orthodoxy. At the time, I don't think any of us knew enough to ask: "But what if her depression was just another symptom of her systemic inflammatory disease, directly related to the high levels of cytokines in her blood?" At the time that would have been regarded as an extraordinarily speculative idea, possibly even a bit bonkers. As a young doctor in training, you don't want senior physicians to start thinking you're bonkers. Maybe that's why I shut up – I sensed that to say any more might take the conversation into career-damaging territory. But, 30 years later, the question is still with me: what if?

What if it was true that Mrs P's depression – her loss of drive and energy, her sadness and guilt, especially about the inconvenience her fatigue was causing to her family and work colleagues – was directly related to bodily inflammation and high levels of cytokines in her blood? Then you'd expect to find that depression was common in many diseases associated with inflammation, not just rheumatoid arthritis.

When I was in medical school, immunological diseases were considered to be rather unusual and obscure. We learnt that systemic lupus erythematosus, or SLE, caused inflammation of the joints (arthritis) and inflammation of the blood vessels (vasculitis) that was somehow related to auto-antibodies targeting the patient's own DNA. We learnt that Hashimoto's thyroiditis caused inflammation of the thyroid gland (as you might have guessed) due to auto-antibodies targeting the patient's own thyroid cells and preventing them from secreting the hormone thyroxine. And we learnt, or tried to learn, lists of scientifically disorganised but diagnostically handy factoids about dozens of other diseases: Sjögren's syndrome caused inflammation of the salivary glands so the patient had a dry mouth; ankylosing spondylitis caused inflammation of the spine so the patient couldn't bend over; Behçet's syndrome caused arthritis and ulceration of the penis; psoriasis caused arthritis and red, raised plaques of inflammation in the skin over the elbows. These and many other things we were taught, so that we could recognise and name the various exotica of immunological disease, in the approved medical lingo, and in almost complete ignorance of what we now know about the biological mechanisms of the immune system.

As immunology has exploded scientifically over the last 20 years or so, we have learnt much more about the causes of diseases, like SLE, that were traditionally but vaguely regarded as somehow immunological in origin. More disruptively, we have also learnt that inflammation and auto-immunity are involved in many disorders that were traditionally considered to have nothing to do with the immune system.

Atherosclerosis, we were taught in the 20th century, was a thickening of the arteries due to deposits of cholesterol just beneath the lining of the arterial walls. If enough cholesterol accumulated it would block the artery completely; and if that artery happened to be supplying blood to the heart, then the patient would have a heart attack. We learnt about it by analogy to plumbing and that was often how it was treated, by a surgical operation to unblock or bypass the blocked piece of arterial pipe. In the 21st century, medical students are taught a significantly different story: the accumulation of cholesterol triggers an inflammatory reaction in the arterial wall. Macrophages, in this case fighting under the *nom de guerre* of foam cells, eat the cholesterol droplets until they are stuffed full of fat, which makes them look foamy under the microscope. And these arterial macrophages do all the other things that macrophages do when they're angry. They spew toxic exhaust causing collateral damage to other cells in the neighbourhood. They pump cytokines into the circulation. They make the inner lining of the artery more sticky or adhesive so that blood cells are more likely to get stuck to it, instead of flowing freely through, progressively forming a clot or thrombus that may block the flow completely. So having a heart attack isn't a random plumbing disaster; it's often the end product of arterial inflammation.

These days it is difficult to think of a disease that isn't caused or complicated by inflammation or auto-immunity. And it is equally difficult to think of a disease that isn't associated with depression, fatigue, anxiety, or some other mental symptom. People who have just had a heart attack, as a result of coronary arterial inflammation, have a 50% risk of depressive symptoms in the following few weeks, amounting to a major depressive episode for about 20%. People with long-term heart disorders also have significantly increased rates of anxiety and depression. And depression is a risk factor for coronary arterial disease and for poor recovery from a heart attack. There is a two-way interaction between depression and heart disease, just as there is between depression and rheumatoid arthritis. Heart disease and arthritis both increase the risk of depression, just as depression worsens the outcome of heart disease and arthritis. If you have diabetes, your risk of depression is at least doubled. People living with multiple sclerosis are three times more likely than normal to suffer a major depressive episode and there is an increased risk of suicide. The list goes on and on: HIV, cancer, stroke, chronic bronchitis, you name it. Pretty much whatever their physical health disorder, patients with long-term medical conditions have increased risk of mental health symptoms, most often depression or fatigue.[20] Mrs P is not alone.

A hard Cartesian might say, over and over again, in the time-honoured fashion: "Well, if I knew I'd got a nasty case of idiosyncratic troglodytis, or whatever, I can imagine that I'd be pretty depressed or anxious or tired too." As always, it's not totally wrong but it's not absolutely or exclusively right. We can also take on board the new knowledge that inflammation is pervasively involved in almost all serious medical disorders. And the mental health symptoms of many patients, like Mrs P, could be directly caused by the same inflammatory mechanisms that cause their physical symptoms.

A bona fide blockbuster

In a post-Cartesian world, it is quite possible that anti-inflammatory drugs could have anti-depressant effects, relieving symptoms of depression, fatigue and "brain fog" in patients with rheumatoid and other inflammatory disorders. Mechanistically, we know that cytokines are released into the circulation and will have inflammatory effects throughout the body, regardless of whether the source of cytokine release is macrophages in an arthritic knee, an atherosclerotic artery, or a rotten tooth. Cytokines are the crucial broadcast media for a focus of inflammation anywhere in the body to be communicated to the central nervous system of the brain. So, we'd expect drugs targeted against cytokines, anti-cytokines, to have particularly potent anti-depressant effects for a patient like Mrs P.

Back in 1989, there were no such drugs. Mrs P had tried many different remedies over the years. On the advice of her learned physicians, she had even tried swallowing small amounts of gold, which now sounds like a potion from the age of alchemy, but was then considered a perfectly respectable treatment for rheumatism. None of the drugs she had taken was very precisely understood in terms of its mechanism of action, in terms of how it worked at a molecular level in the body. None of the drugs was designed specifically to work by disabling cytokines. And as Mrs P knew, but didn't like to complain about too much, none of them worked very well.

Suppose that you wanted to develop a new drug to take out a particular target, a particular cytokine, in the hope that it might do a better job of treating rheumatoid arthritis than any of the existing medicines on offer to a patient like Mrs P. How could you do it? You could follow in the footsteps of Paracelsus and use medicinal chemistry to make hundreds of thousands of candidate drug molecules. You would then need to test each of these would-be drugs to see which of them was most effective at disabling the target cytokine in a test tube. In the pharmaceutical industry, this brute force approach to drug discovery is called high-throughput screening and it is increasingly the work of robots, untiringly and exhaustively testing one candidate drug after another. But even with a lab full of robots, this is a time-consuming process and the end product may be a drug that is good at disabling the cytokine in the lab but not so good at disabling the cytokine in an animal or a human. Or you might end up with a drug that is good at disabling the target cytokine but also (too) good at disabling other proteins that you didn't intend the drug to interfere with. In other words, at the end of a long and winding road of chemical trial-and-error, your best candidate drug might not work as well in patients as it did in the lab, and it may cause side effects because it doesn't selectively take out only the targeted cytokine, but also disables other proteins that are doing no harm and may be important for health. Since the 1980s it has been possible to do better than this in some situations by using an alternative, more biological way of discovering drugs. And, as it happens, one of the first big breakthroughs for this new technology of biopharmaceuticals was the discovery of a new treatment for rheumatoid arthritis.

Once it was clear that rheumatoid arthritis was not primarily a disease of the joints, but a disorder of the immune system, with high levels of cytokines circulating in the blood, inciting self-destructive behaviour by macrophages, it seemed logical to scientists that if a drug could be designed to silence the cytokine signals, it should demobilise the macrophage army and curtail collateral damage to the joints. In principle, an anti-cytokine drug could stop arthritis in its tracks. Attention focused on one cytokine in particular, called tumour necrosis factor, or TNF for short. TNF was identified by immunologists as a plausible drug target for rheumatoid disease; but the next question was how to find an anti-TNF drug that specifically hit that target and disabled that cytokine? The answer to that question also came from immunology.

When a human protein, like TNF, is injected into another animal, like a mouse, the mouse's immune system will recognise the human TNF as an antigen, a non-self protein, and it will react defensively. The mouse will become inflamed and its lymphocytes will start producing antibodies against the human TNF. The mouse's antibodies will bind to the human TNF, effectively eliminating it from the mouse's body within a few days after its injection. The mouse has been vaccinated against human TNF and large amounts of anti-TNF antibodies will continue circulating in its body for many months.

The key biopharmaceutical insight was to see that this natural immune reaction could be leveraged as a biological machine for discovering and manufacturing drugs. Instead of using robots to screen vast numbers of candidate drugs that might or might not work, mice could be used quickly to make antibodies that would certainly and selectively disable human TNF. The anti-TNF antibodies made by the mouse could then be injected back into a patient with rheumatoid arthritis where, theoretically, they should have exactly the same effects as in the mouse, rapidly eliminating human TNF from circulation.

If TNF was indeed a valid target, then hitting it with such a powerful and selective drug as an anti-TNF antibody, should have a therapeutic impact. However, TNF is not the only cytokine implicated in rheumatoid arthritis, it's by no means the only plausible target, and some experts predicted that this strategy of pinpoint-targeting a single molecular signal in the complex communications network of the immune system would fail to work therapeutically. But in fact it worked brilliantly.[21]

Most theoretically plausible ideas about new drugs don't make it. They don't work out in real life for one reason or another. Getting to a new medicine from a biological theory is almost impossible and successful therapeutic innovation had been thin on the ground in rheumatology for decades. But the data from the first clinical trial of anti-TNF antibodies as a new treatment for rheumatoid arthritis were in the slam-dunk zone.[22] Four weeks after they had been randomly assigned to a high or low dose of the anti-TNF drug, or to a placebo, 79% of patients had responded well to high-dose treatment, 44% to the low dose, and only 8% to placebo. The first wave of anti-TNF antibodies commercially launched for the treatment of rheumatoid arthritis – marketed with the brand names of Humera and Remicade – turned into some of the biggest-selling products in the history of the pharmaceutical industry. The immunologists at Charing Cross Hospital in London who had led the first clinical trials in 1992, Marc Feldmann and Ravinder Maini, won a Lasker Prize, one of the Oscars of medicine, in 2003. By 2009, the global market for anti-TNF antibodies was reckoned to be worth more than 20 billion dollars a year. These were bona fide blockbusters in every sense: they made a real difference to many patients; they made a lot of money, because they were truly innovative in both concept and execution; and they unfolded a map, they pioneered a therapeutic strategy that could be customised to chart the critical path of development for other antibody drugs for other immune disorders. The territory opened up by the first biopharmaceuticals for rheumatoid arthritis has since turned into one of the biggest, most productive fields of modern medicine.

The Cartesian blind spot

One might think, given the massive impact of anti-cytokine drugs on the physical symptoms of many inflammatory diseases, that an enormous amount would already be known about their effects on the mental symptoms that Mrs P was telling me about: depression, fatigue and anxiety. One might think, given that many patients with rheumatoid disease rate fatigue as one of their single biggest problems,[17] that a major research effort would by now have been made to understand what beneficial effects anti-cytokine antibodies might have on mental as well as physical symptoms. But one would be wrong.

The first anti-TNF antibodies were available on the NHS as a new medicine for rheumatoid arthritis from 1999, about 10 years after my meeting with Mrs P. I don't know if she tried anti-TNF treatment years later, or whether it made any difference to her depression, or any other aspect of her rheumatoid disease, if she did. I never saw her again after that one meeting. That was my last job in medicine. My next job was my first one as a psychiatrist. I was about to cross the Cartesian line that organisationally divides the medical profession and the NHS. I was about to specialise as a doctor of mind stuff rather than a doctor of physical mechanism. So I never had hands-on experience as a doctor treating patients with anti-TNF antibodies. I never had the chance to see for myself what happens when a patient like Mrs P has her first anti-TNF treatment. But I have spoken to other doctors and nurses who have had that experience and many of them have told me versions of the same story. The patients cheered up, often rapidly. It was so predictable, I was told, that the nurses on the rheumatology ward at University College Hospital in London all wanted to be the one to set up the intravenous drip for an anti-TNF infusion, because they knew the patient would feel better and be full of gratitude almost immediately. It was so predictable, I learnt, that it had a nickname. They called it the Remicade high.

It's exactly what you'd expect if cytokines caused depression: that anti-cytokines should be anti-depressant, that a shot of anti-TNF should make people with inflamed minds feel high. However, despite the fact that it has become part of common parlance in day-to-day clinical practice, the Remicade high has not yet been taken too seriously. It has usually been written off as a placebo response – meaning that if patients were given an innocuous infusion of glucose, but told it was Remicade, they'd still have a Remicade high. Their highness was supposed to be a mental reflection on their prospects of improved physical health following a fancy new treatment. "High? Well you would be, wouldn't you, if you thought that you'd just been treated with a new blockbuster that was going to cure your joint disease?" There have been only a few scientific studies designed to challenge this familiar rigmarole, to test the post-Cartesian hypothesis that patients rapidly feel better after anti-TNF treatment, not because they think positively about the implications of the drug, but because the drug has directly beneficial anti-inflammatory effects on their brain.[23] The Remicade high could be giving us a big clue about a new way of treating depression, fatigue and other symptoms of the inflamed mind, a clue we will investigate later. But so far medicine has mostly discounted it as a trick of the mind. It's another thing hiding in plain sight, camouflaged by our Cartesian blind spot.

⊸⊳⊜ ⊜⊲⊷

In the next chapter, we turn to the world of psychiatry. Traditionally, that changes everything. In a dualist universe, the body and the mind are as different as any two things can be. But as we now pass from one side to the other, as we cross the great divide between those that are sometimes called "proper doctors" and those that are sometimes called "trick cyclists", we will try to keep hold of the inflammatory threads that may in fact tie body and mind together.

Chapter 4

MELANCHOLIA AFTER

DESCARTES

From black bile to MDD

Depression is even more medically ancient than inflammation. We didn't know the cardinal signs of inflammation until the Romans, but melancholia has been a thing since the Greeks. The physicians trained in the school of Hippocrates, about 400 years BC, recognised two facets of melancholia, which we now call emotional and cognitive. They saw an agony of the soul, or *angor animi*, which was expressed by fear, despondency, sadness and gloom. And they described a tendency to form pessimistic and unrealistic beliefs, *cogitatione defixus*, like the patients of Galen "who think they have become a sort of snail so that they must escape everyone in order to avoid having their shell crushed, while others fear that Atlas, who supports the world, may grow weary and vanish".[24]

These emotional and cognitive symptoms were explained physiologically, in terms of abnormal bodily function, by an excessive accumulation in the spleen of black bile. According to Hippocratic physiology, this was one of four humours that were supposed between them to control many aspects of the patient's temperament, susceptibility to disease and response to treatment. Black bile, yellow bile, phlegm and blood were the cardinal humours that circulated throughout the body, their relative balance of influence with respect to each other providing a diagnostic explanation for the clinical appearance of disease. Too much phlegm made a man apathetic and caused rheumatic and chest disease; too much yellow bile made a man angry and more prone to liver disease; too much blood made a man positively sanguine but prone to heart disease; and too much black bile made a man melancholic. The anti-depressant treatments of the time were intended to rebalance the humours, to attenuate the mournful influence of black bile in the body, by diet, exercise, purgatives and bleeding.

Such ancient ideas might seem somewhat ridiculous to us, now that we know there is no such thing as black bile in the body, but they survived for a remarkably long time as the dominant theory of European medicine. English physicians commonly continued to practise in the Hippocratic tradition until the 1850s. And for a melancholic patient a dose of Hippocratic medicine, based on quaintly flawed physiology but physiology nonetheless, would often have been preferable to the alternative treatments based on theology. For example, Celsus, although ancient, was not Hippocratic in his thinking about the root causes of melancholia. Like many people before and since, he regarded it as evidence of demonic possession, a sign that evil spirits had captured the soul of the patient, perhaps as a punishment for wrong-doing or moral laxity. He recommended treatments that were correspondingly severe:

exorcism, beating, burning, solitary confinement, restraint by chains and manacles. From the earliest times, throughout the Middle Ages and into the witch-hunting era of the 18th century, countless melancholics must have been treated with extreme cruelty, sanctioned by the zealous certainty that they suffered not from their bodies but from the devil that was in their souls.

It was only after 1850 that the mechanistic revolution in medicine, penetratingly prophesied by Descartes about 200 years earlier, began to get the upper hand over the Hippocratic tradition. (Change always comes slowly to medicine.) But by the 1950s, the pre-Cartesian, pre-dualist medical theory of the ancients – which explained both mental and physical symptoms by the same underlying humours – the same causative factors or agents – had been almost completely dismantled and replaced by the medicine of the body machine. These days there is only one vestigial fragment of the Hippocratic corpus remaining in the modern medical lexicon. The word melancholia is still in use by psychiatrists, not to denote black bile, but as an alternative diagnostic label for what is now more formally called major depressive disorder (MDD).

Just as the ancient signs of inflammation are still taught to every medical student, the modern syndrome of depression is recognisably the same now as when it was first diagnosed as melancholia 2,000 years ago. But the cardinal features of inflammation have since been deeply explained by the new science of immunology, whereas the clinical symptoms of depression are not yet so well understood at the same level of mechanistic detail. The diagnosis of MDD, as officially defined by the American Psychiatric Association's *Diagnostic and Statistical Manual*, 5th edition (*DSM-5*),[25] involves ticking boxes on a checklist of depressive symptoms that Galen would have recognised, including anhedonia (loss of pleasure) and anorexia (loss of appetite). If a patient has experienced sadness or lack of pleasure, plus at least four of the five other symptoms on the list, almost every day for at least two weeks but not for more than two years, then that patient has MDD, as defined by the committee of eminent psychiatrists who compiled *DSM*. There is no need for any blood tests, physical examinations, X-rays or fMRI scans. According to the *DSM-5* diagnostic algorithm, there is nothing we can learn from the body that would help us make the diagnosis of MDD. Indeed, if blood tests or X-rays indicated that the patient might have a bodily disease that would *unmake* the diagnosis of MDD. By decree of *DSM-5*, a diagnosis of MDD is explicitly excluded if the symptoms could be "attributable to the physiological effects… of another medical condition". So, bizarrely, Mrs P could not have MDD. She could tick all the boxes on the *DSM-5* symptom checklist but her rheumatoid arthritis would rule out the diagnosis of MDD. Depression has officially become isolated on the mental side of the dualist divide, just as inflammation has traditionally been restricted to the physical side.

Who cares? Who cares that depression has been mentally segregated by dualism? What does this rather academic philosophising mean in real life for patients who have depression, and for the psychiatrists and psychologists who treat them?

A cross to bear

For a lot of patients, I believe, it means that depression is likely to be seen as a sign of personal failure. If depression is purely mental, if it's all in the mind, if it's just a different way of feeling, or thinking about things, or behaving, then shouldn't I be as responsible for my depression as I am responsible for other purely mental phenomena, like my ideas and my decisions? Feeling personally culpable, feeling as if it is their fault, is a common experience for depressed people. Clinical psychologists regard this as a cognitive bias, a tendency to think negative rather than positive thoughts about oneself, which is a characteristic feature of depression that can be treated by cognitive behavioural therapy (CBT). But in more severe cases, self-critical or obsessively self-blaming thoughts can drive self-punishing or self-harming behaviours, and ideas of personal failure can morph into nihilistic delusions – the patient's false belief that he has already died. It almost goes without saying that all these self-critically biased states of mind are risk factors for the ultimate auto-destructive act of suicide.

Some degree of psychological assault on one's sense of self, or even one's bodily self in a case of suicide, is thus a central and serious part of the experience of depression for many people. And this has been true for several thousand years, so we can't blame it entirely on Descartes. But I believe that the exclusive segregation of depression to the mental domain – the assumption that it is all in the mind – can exacerbate the sense of guilt that a depressive disorder brings with it, and it can feed the culture of shame and silence that still surrounds depression and other mental health disorders.

It has been said many times, but it is worth repeating, that if my arm is broken I can at least count on the cheerful support of people around me. There will probably be an entertaining story to tell about how it happened, perhaps some thrillingly gory details to share, and other people will generally be happy to listen, to sympathise, to tell in return their own war stories, and to pass on their nuggets of medical advice. But if my mind is broken I can count on none of this. If I am depressed – joyless, hopeless, sleepless and plagued by an incessant sense of worthlessness – I am also much more likely to find myself on my own. I will not be dining out on my unvarnished monologue of despair; people will not be entertained by my story about the funny thing that happened to me in the psychiatric outpatient clinic; they will not be eager to share comparable experiences of their own; the subject will be changed, even my friends may "not know what to say". If I am working, I will probably not want my employer to write the word depression into my HR file. If I am looking for work, I will probably find some alternative facts to explain the several months of sick leave I was forced to take from my previous job. If I am running for public office the disclosure of depression may be enough to derail my campaign. In some countries, if I was hoping to get married, common knowledge of my depression could be enough to trash my eligibility and to blight the marriage prospects of my brothers and sisters, too.

It's called stigma. Jesus of Nazareth was stigmatised by the wounding of his hands and feet when he was crucified; he was physically marked as a common criminal subject to the most degrading and humiliating punishment. The modern stigmatisation of depression and other mental health disorders is not so explicitly brutal. We'd like to think that we have become more civilised and, yes, there has been real progress. We no longer do many of the barbaric things we have done in the past to people with mental illness. But we still prefer not to talk about it. We still don't really know what to say – because if it's all in his or her mind – aren't they personally, poor souls, to blame? In the 21st century, depression is stigmatised not so much by what is done to the patient, by physical wounds or barbaric treatments, as by what is not done or said. We exercise a kind of virtual quarantine, separating the depressed person's experience from ordinary conversation, leaving him or her alone to get over it, to work through it, to pull himself together, to get back to us when she's sorted herself out.

If the dualist isolation of depression in the mind implies a degree of personal blame for causing the problem, it also implies a degree of personal responsibility for finding the solution. Although it may be too shameful to talk about at home or chat about at work, we expect that a certain kind of talking may be exactly what's needed for the patient to understand where their feelings are coming from, to build a narrative, to explain to themselves how they became depressed, what their depression means to them. In the weird world of dualism, we might not know what to say to our friends with depression, we might not want to talk about it with them ourselves, but we are also often adamant that they just need to talk about it with someone, someone who's trained to breach the stigmatised circle of silence.

Super-shrink

For most of the last 100 years or so, it has been common currency that since depression is a disorder of the mind it can and should be cured by the mind. Psychological symptoms need psychological treatment and physical symptoms need physical treatment. It makes perfect sense to a good Cartesian doctor.

The inventor of the world's first psychological treatment was of course Sigmund Freud. I say "of course" because Freud's fame is so extraordinary and the influence of his ideas so extraordinarily enduring.

> If often he was wrong and, at times, absurd,
> To us he is no more a person
> Now but a whole climate of opinion
> Under whom we conduct our different lives.

We are all Freudians now, as Auden said,[26] at least to some degree, whether we like it or not. We all say and do things that issue, however osmotically or obscurely, from the astonishing scope and impact of his analysis. Peak Freud is behind us, no doubt, but he is still the most cited author on Google Scholar, ahead of bibliometric lightweights like Marx and Einstein by a country mile. I remember being awed simply by the sight of the pale-blue spines of the 24 volumes of the Standard Edition of his collected works, lined up on a long shelf in the library of the Institute of Psychiatry in London. The collection of papers and books written by other people about those 24 books by Freud would have filled the entire library.

What has always intrigued me about him was how he got started, and it was not as a psychologist, on the mental side of the Cartesian line. Until his late twenties, Freud aspired to be a brain scientist, a neuroscientist, as we'd now say, working on the physical side of the dualist divide. He was a student of some of the founding fathers of neuroscience and published one of his first papers on the microscopic anatomy, the layout of individual nerve cells, in the spinal cord of "one of the lowest of the fishes". He wrote a paper on aphasia, the loss of language caused by strokes or other pathological lesions of the brain. He conducted many studies on cocaine, often involving self-administration of a supply he had sourced from the drug company Merck in 1884. Freud became one of the first scientists to discover that cocaine rapidly and reversibly numbed the absorbent membranes of the nose and the eye. He could see this was a discovery with medical impact: perhaps cocaine could be used as a local anaesthetic for nose or eye surgery? It was a discovery that could have made him a star. But, at a crucial moment, he was lured away from his studies to spend a holiday with his fiancée. By the time he returned from this happy hiatus, another (now forgotten) scientist had demonstrated that cocaine could be used as a surgical anaesthetic for eye operations on animals, depriving Freud of the public glory of his discovery. As he later remarked, I think ironically, "it was the fault of my fiancée that I was not already famous... but I bore [her] no grudge for the interruption".[27] They married and settled down in 1886.

Over the next 10 years, his life switched tracks. Freud knew that the career path of a serious neuroscientist to a professorial chair in the University of Vienna was not open to him, because he was Jewish, although he would have been a strong candidate on merit. He had to spend more time away from the laboratory doing private medical practice to support his wife and family. And his professional relationships became concentrated on intense intellectual "congress" with just a few key peers or comrades, like Josef Breuer and Wilhelm Fliess.

Breuer was an older man, who had already won the high medical accolade of having a bit of the human body named after him (and his colleague, Ewald Hering). Together they had discovered the Hering-Breuer reflex, which slows down your heart rate when you take a deep breath. You can try this at home. Sitting quietly, feel the pulse at your wrist, and count the number of heartbeats in a 30-second period (which should be about 35). Then inhale deeply and hold your breath for 30 seconds, with your chest fully expanded, while you take your pulse again. Then breathe out while still feeling your pulse. You should have found that while your lungs were fully inflated your heart rate slowed down; and then it speeded up when you started breathing normally again. That is the Hering-Breuer reflex in action. Inflation of the lungs quickly, automatically, reflexively slows down the heart rate by sending a signal through the vagus nerve. It is one example of the many ways in which the vagus nerve mediates connections between the brain and the body. But Breuer's later work with Freud focused instead on hypnosis for the treatment of hysterical symptoms in young women and resulted in their joint publication of a series of case histories in 1895.

Fliess was younger, less respectable and less scientifically distinguished than Breuer, but perhaps more liberating creatively for Freud. He was a "brilliant but unbalanced" surgeon in Berlin, who used cocaine enthusiastically as an anaesthetic for operations on the nose, and had an almost mystical interest in the significance of biorhythms, like the menstrual cycle, that oscillated over periods of 23 or 28 days. For about 15 years after they first met in 1887, Fliess and Freud corresponded extensively and conspired to develop a naso-genital theory according to which neurotic or hysterical symptoms originating in the female genitals could be treated by applying cocaine to the nose, or even by a surgical operation on the nose.[28]

It was on the train back to Vienna, after visiting Fliess for several days in Berlin in September 1895, perhaps just as his carriage was jolted as it passed over some points in the track, that Freud began to write an essay that crystallised his intellectual switching of tracks from the brain to the mind. He dashed off 40,000 words in a few weeks and urgently sent them to Fliess; how Fliess responded we don't know because Freud later destroyed all the letters he'd received from him. We do know that years later, when Freud's passion had cooled to the point that the name Fliess wasn't mentioned in his autobiography, Freud tried to destroy the only extant copy of the manuscript. It was smuggled out of Nazi Germany by a circuitous route and eventually published in 1950, entitled *Project for a Scientific Psychology.*[29] It is the raw manifesto of psychoanalysis. All the pale-blue volumes in the Institute of Psychiatry library originated from this unfinished and very nearly unpublished blueprint.

Freud conceived of an elusive psychic energy, which obeyed

the physical laws of motion yet was not measurable, as it flowed through chains and circuits of nerve cells, its direction of travel determining the content of consciousness. He illustrated his idea in one of the very few diagrams or graphics he ever incorporated in his prolific output of words (Fig. 5). It was a most audacious effort to reach across the Cartesian divide from his neuroscientific base on the body side to the terra incognita on the mind side. Freud never tested or supported his idea by any laboratory experiments and, given the technological state of neuroscience at the time, he wouldn't have succeeded even if he'd tried. Freud's *Project* aspired to create a new science of the mind based on the emerging science of the brain – and he coined the new word psychoanalysis to summarise this revolutionary agenda – but it did not play out like that. Psychoanalysis might have been first imagined by Freud as a point of connection between the domains of the mind and the body but it subsequently departed ever more completely to the mental side.

Patients talked and Freud listened. Patients didn't talk and Freud listened to that too. As he listened to what his patient was or was not saying, he also listened to himself. It was all in the minds of the two of them, in the dialectic of transference and counter-transference. The psychoanalytic relationship became Freud's new lab. It was in those hours and hours of consultation that he heard or inferred the raw material that he assembled into the books that made him world-famous. Unchained from its original coupling to the brain, psychic energy in the form of libido freely suffused his theories. Libido had a life story that dated back to birth and the infant's first relationships with its mother and father.

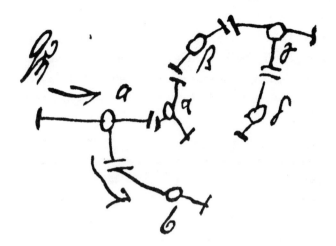

Figure 5: Freud's first draft of the ego. Psychic energy, or libido, signified by a cryptic glyph that looks a bit like a Q for quantity, enters this schematic brain and flows from one nerve cell to another. The direction of flow is dictated by the resistance of the gaps between nerve cells and by the extent to which cells are already charged with energy. Freud imagines that the first nerve cell, a, represents a hostile memory. As that cell is activated by psychic energy an unpleasant memory will come to mind. The libidinal energy could then automatically flow through the first cell to activate a second cell, b, a nerve cell for unpleasure or sadness. Alternatively, the group of nerve cells labelled α, β, γ, δ – which Freud called the ego – may already be sufficiently charged with energy to divert the incoming quantum of psychic energy in their direction, away from the unpleasure cell, thus inhibiting the sad feelings that would otherwise be triggered by a hostile memory. It is his original map of a psychological defence mechanism, the ego suppressing subconsciously revoked emotional pain, projected onto the cutting edge neuroscience of his day. Freud's visionary sketch admits no doubt even about the existence of synaptic gaps between cells, although at the time no one, not even the great Ramón y Cajal, could actually see them (Fig. 8).

Libidinal development could be interrupted or perturbed by the quality of the child's relationship with its parents, or by the child's real or fantasised exposure to sexual abuse. Libido could animate consciousness and it could also abide unconsciously, lurking beneath the surface of the mind as a charge of psychic energy attached to traumatic but forgotten memories, furtively driving the formation of symptoms as a twisted alternative to the pain of reliving in adult life the unbounded humiliations and deprivations of childhood. It was the work of psychoanalysis to seek out these libidinal depth charges, buried deep in the mind, and to discharge them cathartically, to release libidinal energy from its infantile attachments and so to relieve the unconscious pressure to make symptoms.

Freud liked to think that he navigated his intellectual journey from the lab bench to the couch in "splendid isolation". Psychoanalysis was uniquely and entirely his discovery, by an act of heroic self-analysis, and anyone else wishing to become a psychoanalyst must first be analysed by Freud himself, or by someone who had been analysed by Freud. The profession of psychoanalysis was originally constituted like a family, with each analyst dynastically related through their own analysis to the patriarchal authority of Freud. But as the family grew larger it became more fractious and schismatic. Psychoanalytic theory diversified into different species and subspecies, each with their own distinctive jargon and preoccupations, each motivating a different type of what became known generically as psychotherapy.

These days, a patient seeking treatment for depression in the NHS is unlikely to be inducted into the Freudian lineage by old school psychoanalysis. It takes too long, it's too expensive and there's never been much evidence that it works for the theoretical reasons it's supposed to work, or that it works much better than any other flavour of psychotherapy.[30] Most studies have shown that psychological treatment (of some sort) for depression is better than nothing, on average, and that for some people it can be very effective. But it doesn't seem to matter too much whether it's Freud's psychoanalysis, Jung's analytical psychology, Beck's cognitive therapy, or another charismatically advocated brand. The best predictor of therapeutic response is not the therapist's training background, or what's written in the standard treatment manuals, but the quality of their personal relationship with the patient, the strength of the therapeutic alliance between them. Simply finding someone to talk to, someone who knows, or at least thinks they know, what to say and what not to say, someone thereby empowered to break the circle of silence, may be the most important ingredient of successful psychotherapy for many patients.

Stigmatisation and psychotherapy are both strongly motivated by the Cartesian divide, by the isolation of depression as a disorder purely of the mind. They are both everyday experiences of living with depression that are conditioned by or compliant with the medically orthodox ideology – we could call it the MOI position – that mind is distinct from body. We might think of stigmatisation as bad and psychotherapy as good but they are equally to be expected in a dualistic world. Much less predictably ordained by the Cartesian settlement, but nonetheless now a matter of routine clinical practice, is the widespread use of anti-depressant drugs.

In an ideal world, purely illuminated by the light of

Cartesian reason, Prozac should never have happened.

Dancing in the sanatorium

Drugs are molecules, collections of atoms, tiny pieces of the physical world, that work by targeting and perturbing the biochemical machinery of the body. The existence of drugs that could have beneficial effects on depression, or any other undesirable mental state, is inconceivable to the extent that you are a hard Cartesian. If you are a radically divisive dualist, who thinks that one's thought can have nothing to do with anything at all in the physical world, who believes, like Descartes, that the soul can survive the death of the body, then psychoactive drugs are logically impossible. How could targeting a brain or body mechanism for drug treatment make sense if the symptoms are caused by the turbulence of "animal spirits"? It would be like trying to tune a musical instrument by looking at it, rather than listening to it.

But, in fact, as we all know, many psycho-active drugs exist and have been widely used for various purposes by *Homo sapiens* for ever. Alcohol, opiates, psilocybin, cannabinoids and atropine are among the mind-altering drugs that early humans discovered in plants and used for prehistoric sacred or healing rituals for about 100,000 years before Hippocrates. The written Hippocratic corpus then prescribed abundant and creative use of medicinal herbs to rebalance temperamental humours throughout the ancient and middle ages. In 17th-century cities like London, the guilds or societies of apothecaries, who specialised in horticulture and the formulation of herbal remedies, were commercially prosperous and professionally ambitious organisations. Sir Hans Sloane, having made a fortune from London property investments and Jamaican sugar plantations, built a beautiful garden for the Apothecaries' Company in 1673. It was situated close to the river Thames in Chelsea, where he was lord of the manor, so that it was easy for new plants to be shipped in from all over the world. The garden was used to describe, catalogue and investigate freshly imported plants, many of them never before seen by science, from Asia Minor, the Caribbean, America, China and South Africa. Plants were carefully evaluated for their beneficial or useful properties as foods, as sources of fibre for clothing material, and as medicines. It might have seemed to Sloane, the shrewd investor that he was, that nothing could possibly go wrong with this buccaneering business model. Opportunities for research-and-development-led innovation and global sales growth must have beckoned from all angles to a forward-thinking 17th-century apothecary in London. And Sloane was right. Herbal remedies for Hippocratic distempers was a good business, for about 200 years; until about 1850, when Hippocratic theory collapsed under the growing mass of discoveries about the body machine, and herbal remedies began to be seriously challenged and overtaken by the innovation in chemical drugs.

The success of the Sloane business model, while it lasted, was sustained in the face of torrential sarcasm and incredulity from its ultimate customers, the patients. People who had to consult 17th- and 18th-century physicians, even in sophisticated European cities like Paris, had little hope of coming away any the wiser about the cause of their disease. Physicians were notorious for their impenetrable professional babble, a mumbo-jumbo of non sequiturs and circularity, obscured by as many Greek and Latin words as possible. Satirists like Voltaire and Molière filled theatres with their dark comedies about medical buffoonery, venality and lethality.

Molière must have consulted many physicians, sometimes desperately and against his better judgment, because at the peak of his career he was in the process of dying from consumption, as tuberculosis (TB) was then called. He would have heard physicians pontificate to him and contend with each other; he knew their combination of pomposity and incompetence very well. At the start of *Le malade imaginaire*,[31] a comedy-ballet he composed as a *divertissement* for King Louis XIV, the curtain rises on a shepherdess, singing sweetly:

Doctors, your learning is purely illusion
Your remedies rubbish, your order confusion
Your big Latin words are unable to cure
This sickening sadness I have to endure
So from my sorrow, one thing is sure;
Doctors, your learning is simply absurd.

Before it was scientifically diagnosed as TB and antibiotics were available to treat it, many men and women would die of consumption, like Molière. But he was perhaps the only man in history to do so on stage. For the Parisian *début* of this new and final play of his, Molière himself played the central part of the hypochondriac. On the fourth night of the opening production, he started coughing up gouts of blood, for real, the spreading red stains on his green satin costume clearly visible even from the cheapest seats. He collapsed in front of his audience and died a few hours later. It was, for one night only, the ultimate *coup de théâtre* in his life-long campaign against Hippocratic medicine.

You might ask yourself, if things were really as bad as Molière was saying, why were any of the fashionable Parisian theatre-goers who thronged to his plays still consulting these ludicrous physicians? Once he'd told them the truth about their doctors they could have walked away; but instead they laughed. They couldn't walk away. Even the most discerning customers couldn't kill the business model, because they had nowhere else to go, and, sure as hell, they were going to get sick at some point. The Hippocratic business was robust to any amount of reputational risk while it was the only game in town. But it imploded completely in the face of competition, once chemical as well as herbal medicines began to be available to patients.

Being a supremely well-connected physician and scientist, Sir Hans Sloane would probably have heard of the first prophet of doom for his business model, even as he was investing in the Chelsea Physic Garden in the 1670s. The prophet's real name was Philippus Aureolus Theophrastus Bombastus von Hohenheim but when he was about 30, in the 1520s, he started calling himself Paracelsus. His father was a Swiss physician and he was apprenticed in medicine and alchemy from an early age. He was self-confident, talented, perfectly poised for a conventional medical career. But he would not allow himself to be trained, or licensed, in the Hippocratic tradition. He publicly burnt copies of the ancient corpus, criticised apothecaries for selling hocus-pocus potions, and despised academic physicians. He deliberately outraged the medical authorities in every city he visited; and so he was driven from Basel to Zurich, from Zurich to Heidelberg, from city to city, all his life. He thought of himself as a radical reformer of medicine on the same scale as Martin Luther was a reformer of the Church. Instead of four Hippocratic humours, he modestly proposed three Paracelsian elements (sulphur, mercury and salt) and he used these as the principal ingredients in his chemical remedies.

When he wandered into Nuremberg in 1529, the local physicians were goaded by his taunts and sneers to challenge him to cure the incurable: 15 patients with the French disease, as the ongoing plague of syphilis was then known by German-speaking people. Paracelsus visited the patients in the leper colony, where they were held outside the town walls, and it was almost miraculous what he did – the skin ulcers and sores of the syphilitic patients vanished (or at least some of them did) – thanks to his innovative and secretive use of a mercury ointment. It wasn't quite the cure he said it was. Mercury killed the syphilitic germs that it contacted on the skin – which helped the visible ulcers heal – but there were many untreated and invisible germs in the body that his ointment couldn't reach. Still, it was good enough to get him safely out of Nuremberg and back on the open road, where 12 years later he was killed in a drunken brawl outside Salzburg (Fig. 6).

Paracelsus died penniless and without honour in his own time, but he did foresee the future correctly in some ways.

Figure 6: First prophet of pharmaceuticals. Paracelsus was neither pretty nor manly looking. He never married and he couldn't grow a beard. It is said that he might have suffered a nasty case of mumps before puberty, which infected and destroyed his testes. But his personal motto, inscribed in the border in this image, was defiantly self-assertive: "Let no man belong to another who can belong to himself." He is surrounded by occult symbols of his hermetic knowledge, like the Rosicrucian motif of a child's head emerging from the landscape visible through the window behind him. And he is clutching with both hands his immense sword of mysterious provenance, called Azoth, a magic word for the force of nature. You'd never guess from this composed and esoteric portrait but Paracelsus was notoriously argumentative when drunk, and quick to start slashing the air with Azoth to make his points even clearer to the idiots with whom he was debating. Experts believe this may have had something to do with his violent death in a tavern at the age of 48. Those of us living after Freud might also think of the mighty Azoth as a phallic symbol compensating for his lived experience of castration.

Three hundred years after his death, in the second half of the 19th century, the Hippocratic establishment he'd raged against all his life was finally collapsing in the face of Cartesian medicine. And the first pharmaceutical companies, like Merck and Roche, had begun using chemistry rather than alchemy to discover, purify, measure and manufacture drugs. A new industry began to grow from chemical and dye companies, many of them founded in cities like Basel, that had been much frequented by Paracelsus. The pharmaceutical industry was getting organised to do what he had tried to do in his alchemical workshop, but big time, and with the benefit of better science.

The first breakthrough pharmaceuticals were the new wonder drugs for infectious diseases that started appearing on the market in the first half of the 20th century. Paracelsus's mercury cure for syphilis, which was often as dangerous to the patient as the disease, was supplanted by more effective and less toxic chemical drugs from about 1910. Penicillin – the first antibiotic pharmaceutical – proved to be extremely effective and safe as a treatment for syphilis and other infections from the 1940s. Other new antibiotic drugs were produced for the treatment of TB in the 1940s and 1950s, including one that eventually and unexpectedly opened up a huge pharmaceutical business for the treatment of depression. The age of Prozac originated accidentally from this great wave of innovation in antibiotics.

To develop the new anti-TB drugs, companies like Roche followed a scientifically logical path. They screened many different molecules in the lab to see which of them was most effective at killing the germ that was known to be the root cause of the disease, called *Mycobacterium tuberculosis*. They reasoned correctly that if you could find a chemical that killed these bacteria in a test tube, or in an experimentally infected mouse, there was a good chance it might also kill them in the human body and cure the disease. It so happened, at the end of World War II, that a large stockpile of a chemical called hydrazine, which had been produced by the Germans as rocket fuel for planes and flying bombs, was liberated by the Allies for pharmaceutical research. Roche synthesised hundreds of new molecules based on hydrazine and screened them for efficacy in mice infected with the TB germ. They found one molecule, called iproniazid, that stopped the bacteria from reproducing and it prolonged the lifespan of infected mice. The next step was to test whether it actually worked in patients, and to do this Roche started a clinical trial.

At the start of the 20th century, TB, known as the white plague, was the second-commonest cause of death in New York and in 1913 the city opened a vast hospital exclusively for patients with the disease on a secluded plot on Staten Island. Sea View Hospital was designed partly as a sanatorium for patients to rest, to enjoy fresh air, sunlight and uplifting views of the ocean; and partly as a prison to keep them isolated from the rest of the population while their disease remorselessly progressed, despite the scenery, to the point of death. There was no effective treatment. Patients spent their days lying listlessly on their beds, wasting away, depressed and exhausted, waiting for things to get even worse. The clinical trial of iproniazid at Sea View Hospital in 1952 burst upon this dismal scene with awesome power. Patients were immediately energised by the drug, they became much more active and sociable, much hungrier, and their lung disease was stopped in its tracks (Fig. 7). For the first time, patients began to leave Sea View Hospital while still alive, and return to a normal life in the city. The wards were almost completely deserted by the early 1960s and most of what's left of the hospital today is a grim ruin, designated as a site of historical interest.

The golden age

There's never been much doubt about the impact of iproniazid, and the other wonder drugs of its generation, on the treatment of TB. This was truly a miracle cure, as the newspapers said, built on solid science, as physicians knew. But it was not so obvious what to make of the euphoria unexpectedly caused by iproniazid. Good Cartesian doctors argued that it must be a placebo effect. Many of the early clinical trials were not properly blinded or controlled, meaning that patients knew they were going to be given a drug that they believed could cure them. And if you thought that you were going to be reprieved from a sentence of death by the white plague, well, you'd cheer up, wouldn't you? But some doctors thought that there could be more to the dancing in the wards than just a placebo effect; they thought it might be a serendipitous clue to hitherto unsuspected actions of this anti-TB drug on the human brain.

Like every other up-and-coming psychiatrist in New York in the 1950s, Nathan Kline would have been well aware

Figure 7: Scenes of joy at the dawn of anti-depressants. *Life* magazine ran a photo story in 1952, capturing the happy, smiling faces of patients who had been written off as hopeless TB cases, consigned to death at the hands of the white plague, until they were enrolled in a clinical trial of iproniazid. A wave of euphoria swept through the wards and patients were "dancing in the halls tho' there were holes in their lungs" as they celebrated their new lease on life. They were lucky enough to be treated with one of the first effective anti-tuberculosis drugs that, surprisingly, also turned out to be the world's first anti-depressant.

that he was conducting his professional life in a climate of Freudianism. Psychoanalysis was close to its high tide mark as the dominant school of thought in American psychiatry at the time. But Kline was interested in the very different approach to treatment of depression suggested by the Sea View TB trials. So he talked about iproniazid as a "psychic energiser", as if it might work by tickling up the depressed libido, just like psychoanalysis, but in a tablet not on a couch. He was the leader of a small group of psychiatrists who conducted the first clinical trials to test the drug in patients who were depressed without also having TB.[32] In 1957, they reported that they had given the drug to 24 patients, about 18 of whom had shown improvements in their mood and social engagement as a result of treatment for five weeks. There was no experimental control for a possible placebo effect and most of the patients had a diagnosis of schizophrenia, not depression. Nowadays results like these would be regarded as embarrassingly flimsy evidence for anti-depressant efficacy. But less than a year later, 400,000 depressed patients had been treated with iproniazid, despite the fact that it was officially licensed at the time only for TB; and Kline had secured the personal support of the President of Roche to license and market it for depression. Seven years later, iproniazid had been joined on the market by about 10 other new anti-depressant drugs and more than 4 million patients had been treated. Kline picked up the lucrative Lasker Prize in 1964, and was tipped for the Nobel, because "more than any other psychiatrist [he] has been responsible for one of the greatest revolutions ever to occur in the care and treatment of the mentally ill".[33] One of the colleagues who'd helped Kline do the clinical trials didn't see things quite the same way and took him to court for half of the kudos and half of the $10,000 cash. Kline paid up. The call from Stockholm never came.

Amid the booming sales and the vertiginous career moves of the protagonists, it is important to remember that the question of how, exactly, iproniazid worked as an anti-depressant was not settled. "Psychic energiser" might usefully mean a lot of different things to a lot of different people but scientifically it was a travesty. How could a drug, a physical thing, impart some quasi-libidinal energy to the psyche? There had to be a better explanation of how iproniazid worked in terms of the physical or chemical mechanisms of the brain, at least as far as those mechanisms were currently understood. And at the time – the early 1960s – there was a lot of excitement about the synaptic mechanisms by which nerve cells communicated with each other. The buzzwords of the day were the names of so-called neurotransmitters such as dopamine and adrenaline, together known as catecholamines. Enterprising psychiatrists, seeking a non-psychic mechanism of action for iproniazid and other anti-depressants, forged from this new neuroscience some highly influential theories about how anti-depressant drugs worked and about what causes depression in the first place. But to understand where those theories came from and how they led to Prozac, we first have to step back a bit.

We take it for granted now that in the human brain there are about 100 billion nerve cells that must work together as a system, the central nervous system. Clearly, communication between individual cells must be very important in enabling them to function as a system. But how are nerve cells connected to each other? The first person to start answering this question correctly was a Spanish contemporary of Freud's, called Santiago Ramón y Cajal, who is now widely regarded as the founding father of modern neuroscience. He was an extremely skilled microscopist, who was able to use new staining techniques to highlight individual nerve cells, to isolate them visually from the mass of surrounding nervous tissue, so that when he looked down the microscope he could see the intricacies of each cell in minute detail. Very few people had ever seen the nervous system in this light before, one of whom was Camillo Golgi, the professor of anatomy at Padua, who had earlier invented the microscopic staining techniques that Ramón y Cajal was using.

As well as being able to see such almost unprecedented sights, which was no mean feat in itself, Ramón y Cajal was also able to draw what he saw with great precision and artistry. And he was a workaholic. He single-handedly produced an enormous number of microscope slides and drawings of nerve cells, each executed to the highest possible standard. He published magisterial papers and text-books on the vertebrate brain that encompassed humans and many other animals, at all stages of development, in health and disease (Fig. 8). And his authoritative view was that nerve cells often made very close contact with each other, but they remained individually distinct, meaning there must be a space or a gap between even the closest pair of cells. This was a bold claim to make, for such a scrupulous observer of nature, because Ramón y Cajal could not actually see a gap. He reasoned that it must be too narrow to be visible at the highest magnification that 19th-century microscopes could provide.

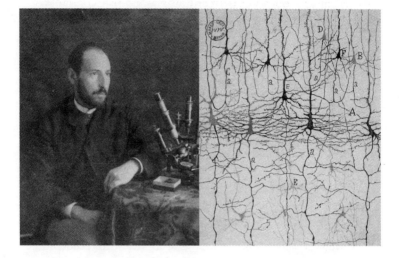

Figure 8: The seer and the synapse. As a boy, Santiago Ramón y Cajal most wanted to be an artist but was persuaded by his father to become a physician, which he dutifully did although he didn't like it. As a young man, he used his artistic talent to produce stunningly beautiful and accurate pen-and-ink drawings of the nerve cells he saw clearly for the first time, using a brass microscope on an old kitchen table. He could see individual cells made very close contact with each other, to form a network of nerve cells. Where two cells contacted each other, not even he could see a gap between them. But he was convinced that a gap existed and in the 1950s, about 20 years after he died, he was vindicated. It is now taken as a matter of fact that there is a synaptic gap, bridged by neurotransmitters like serotonin, between nerve cells that are closely contiguous but not continuous (Fig. 10).

Not everyone agreed with him: Golgi for one. When Golgi looked down the microscope, like Ramón y Cajal, he saw that there were countless densely stained nuclei in nervous tissue, and thin strands of cytoplasm forming an intricate tracery between the nuclear bodies. And like Ramón y Cajal, Golgi couldn't see a gap or a space that marked a boundary between one cell and another. But to Golgi that meant that there wasn't a gap. If it is was invisible it couldn't be there. He described what he saw as a single continuous web, or syncytium, of nervous tissue. And he had some sharp questions for Ramón y Cajal. Why should we believe that there is a gap between nerve cells when we can't see it? And if there is a gap between cells, even an invisibly narrow one, how do the cells communicate with each other? The Nobel Prize committee couldn't decide who was right: in 1906, Golgi and Ramón y Cajal were jointly awarded the prize for their equally brilliant work and mutually contradictory theories. It was only about 40 years later, after both men had died, when electron microscopes were used for the first time to look at nerve cells with much greater magnification than the old light microscopes, that the synaptic gap between nerve cells, which Ramón y Cajal had always known was there, swam sharply into focus.

That dealt with the first of Golgi's objections – we didn't have to believe in an invisible gap any more – but it made his second question all the more pressing. Now that we know a gap exists, how can nerve cells communicate across it? The synaptic gap is typically less than a thousandth of a millimetre from one nerve cell to another. That's very narrow but it's not nothing. It's still a gap, filled by a watery solution of salts and molecules that will be resistant to the passage of an electric current. So the electrical impulses that carry information from one end to another of a single nerve cell can't simply carry on through the synaptic gap, as if it wasn't there, to electrically activate the next-door cell. Somehow the electrical signal has to be converted into a different kind of signal that can bridge the gap, or pass the baton, to communicate between two nerve cells.

We now know that synapses bridge the gap by chemical signalling. The upstream nerve cell produces chemical messengers, called neurotransmitters, and releases them into the synaptic gap when it is electrically stimulated. These chemicals quickly diffuse across the gap and bind to receptors on the surface of the downstream cell, triggering its electrical activation. That's how the electrical signal jumps from one nerve cell to another. In the 1950s, it was becoming clear that the brain used many different neurotransmitters for this purpose. There wasn't a one-word answer to Golgi's second question, about how nerve cells communicated with each other. Some synaptic gaps were bridged by adrenaline molecules, while other nerve cells used noradrenaline, or dopamine, or serotonin, as a neurotransmitter.

When scientists started thinking about what iproniazid might be doing in the brain that could explain its euphoriant and anti-depressant effects, they realised that the drug could boost signalling across synaptic gaps between nerve cells that used adrenaline or noradrenaline as chemical messengers. Iproniazid inhibited an enzyme that broke down adrenaline after it was released into the synaptic gap, effectively turning off the chemical signal soon after it had been turned on. By inhibiting its normal breakdown, iproniazid prolonged and intensified the effect of adrenaline in the synapse. Could this be its mechanism of action as an anti-depressant drug? The answer seemed to be yes for iproniazid and yes, more generally, for all the other new drugs that had followed iproniazid into the rapidly growing market for anti-depressants. Remarkably, they all turned out, one way or another, to boost the effects of synaptic transmission mediated by adrenaline or noradrenaline, collectively known as catecholamines.

It all seemed to fit together. In 1965, Joseph Schildkraut, later to become a professor of psychiatry at Harvard, published an influential paper that took the next step.[34] His title said it all: "The catecholamine hypothesis of affective disorders". Given that anti-depressant drugs boosted the effects of adrenaline and noradrenaline, he argued that the reason patients were depressed in the first place was that they didn't have enough catecholamines in their brains. This might not seem like a great leap, but it is.

Schildkraut was proposing that adrenaline and noradrenaline not only explained the mechanism of action of anti-depressants – how the drugs worked – but were also the fundamental cause of depression. Drugs like iproniazid were imagined not just to increase the availability of key neurotransmitters but to restore their normal levels in the brain, to rescue depressed patients from a hitherto unrecognised condition of brain adrenaline or noradrenaline deficiency. His article was admirably nuanced. He did not over-sell the idea. He offered it as a heuristic, not a matter of fact, and he was well aware that there was very little evidence that depressed patients did indeed have reduced levels of catecholamine signalling before they were treated with anti-depressant drugs. But it must have seemed to him and his contemporaries that it was only a matter of time before that last piece of the puzzle slotted into place. What was by then known as the psycho-pharmacological revolution had moved so far, so fast, from there being no effective drugs in 1955 to dozens in 1965, that another turn of the wheel must surely be enough to drive psychiatry forward to complete enlightenment.

Scientists working for Eli Lilly, an American pharma company, thought they knew what to do next.[35] They assumed that Schildkraut's theory was correct, so far as it went, but not complete. They knew that adrenaline and noradrenaline were not the only neurotransmitters in the brain: there was also serotonin. They started from the idea that serotonin was a plausible new target for anti-depressant drug development. Then they discovered molecules that could boost serotonin transmission, by blocking its reuptake from the synaptic gap, and called them selective serotonin reuptake inhibitors (or SSRIs for short). By the mid-1970s they were ready to put their lead molecule – their best SSRI – into a clinical trial for depression. But the senior management of the company wasn't convinced it would work and financed only a small-scale study. It failed. The patients treated with the SSRI were no less depressed at the end of the trial than the patients treated with a placebo, an anodyne sugar pill. The scientists who had been working on it, for a decade by then, pushed on. They believed passionately that their drug must work for depression because, unlike the accidental discoveries of iproniazid and its ilk, the development of SSRIs was based on a mechanistic rationale from the outset. They thought there was a reason to believe, a reason to look through the unwelcome news of a single failed trial, and to try again. In its subsequent trials, their SSRI was significantly more effective than the placebo. By 1987, it was licensed as a new anti-depressant and marketed under the brand name of Prozac.

It meteorically attained a rock star status unlike any other psychiatric drug before or since. In 1990, Prozac was on the cover of *Newsweek*. By 1995, it was generating two billion dollars of sales worldwide and *Prozac Nation*[36] was the title of a best-selling memoir of life with depression. By 2000, it had been prescribed to about 40 million patients and *Fortune* magazine had listed it as one of the products of the century. But, in the perfect light of hindsight, the launch of Prozac was the blazing sunset, not the dawn, of the golden age of anti-depressants. In the 30 years following the seminal and surprising observation that an antibiotic caused outbreaks of dancing in a TB sanatorium, industrial and academic researchers collectively produced many new drugs, and many new theories about how they worked. In the 30 years following Prozac, the field has not flourished but fizzled out. There have been no major new advances in drug treatment, or psychological treatment come to that, for depression or any other mental health disorder, since about 1990. I'll say that again.

When I started specialist training as a 29-year-old psychiatrist, at St George's Hospital and then the Bethlem Royal and Maudsley Hospital, in London in 1989, it was recommended we study a couple of standard textbooks that covered all the major theories and therapeutics that were then considered important for psychiatry. To this day, in 2018, I could still safely and acceptably treat most patients with mental health disorders based solely on what was written in those textbooks. That would not be true for my contemporaries who special-ised in different areas of medicine at the same time as I went into psychiatry. If I was an oncologist, or cancer physician, who treated cancer patients in 2018 within the limits of what was known about cancer biology and anti-cancer treatment in 1989, I would be struck off for malpractice. Likewise, if I was a rheumatologist treating patients today without knowledge of anti-TNF (tumour necrosis factor) antibodies, or if I was a neurologist treating patients in ignorance of recent advances in immunological treatment of multiple sclerosis.[37] In most other areas of medicine, the last 35 years have witnessed suffi-cient scientifically driven change in theory to reveal that what was known in 1989 may not have been completely wrong but it is certainly not good enough for clinical practice in 2018. Only in psychiatry has time apparently stood still. What we had for depression when I started – SSRIs and psychotherapy – is pretty much still all that we've got therapeutically. They are both modestly effective on average and more markedly beneficial for some patients. They're OK. But no major new treatments for depression – or any other mental health disorder – have been introduced since the sun of Prozac sank beneath the horizon of progress.

Farcical serotonin

How did it all go wrong? The short answer is from the begin-ning. The germ of the problem was the lack of a germ. The development of iproniazid as a cure for TB was correctly predicated on the identification of *Mycobacterium tuberculosis* as the germ that caused the disease. Iproniazid was selected from hundreds of other candidate drugs because of its exceptional ability to stop these bacteria from multiplying in a Petri dish or in a mouse. Then it was shown to be effective in patients who were infected with the same bacteria. The scientific logic proceeded securely from a well-validated drug target to a clinically successful medicine. By comparison, the development of iproniazid as a drug for depression was logically back to front. The path started with a clinical effect (elation in TB patients); worked back from that to decide that the drug target was an enzyme that controls the amount of adrenaline in the brain; and then worked back from that to infer that depressed people must have low levels of adrenaline. For TB, the drug was engineered to treat the disease, whereas, for depression, the disease was reverse-engineered to fit the drug.

The development path of Prozac was logically more respectable. The scientists at Lilly started from a target, serotonin, that they thought was a causative factor in depression, based on the high-profile neurotransmitter theories of the time. They worked forward from that starting point to find a drug that hit the target (and only the target); and then they demonstrated that the drug (sometimes) worked in clinical trials. That progression from target to drug to clinical trial is the tried-and-tested path of drug development. It works well if you start from the right place, by picking the right target, a valid target. But if you start from the wrong place, by picking an invalid target, a molecule or a cell or a germ that doesn't really have anything to do with the disease you're trying to treat, then following the correct path can still lead you into trouble.

Even as Schildkraut unveiled his new theory of depression he pointed out that there was a hole in it. There was very little evidence in 1965 that patients with depression had abnormal levels of adrenaline or noradrenaline in their brains. The same was true of serotonin when the Lilly scientists started their hunt for the first SSRI about 1975. It was a drug target, fair enough, but not a well-validated one. Medicinal chemistry had advanced to the point that it was increasingly easy to engineer drugs that were designed specifically to disable serotonin reuptake inhibitors, and only serotonin reuptake inhibitors. LY110140, as Prozac was known in the Lilly labs before it became world-famous, had good pharmacology. It hit the target pretty cleanly. But there was never much evidence that serotonin was the right target to be hitting in every patient with depression; and there still isn't.

We know that serotonin is biologically ancient; it exists in every nervous system, stretching back in evolutionary time from *Homo sapiens* to the humble worm, *Caenorhabditis elegans*. Regardless of the species of animal, the number of nerve cells that manufacture and release serotonin is generally very small compared to the number of nerve cells that have serotonin receptors on their surface. In the worm brain, there are only three nerve cells that make serotonin but hundreds of nerve cells that are sensitive to it.[38] In the human brain, the serotonin-producing nerve cells are clustered together to form two small nuclei in the brain stem, one of the most primitive parts of the brain, close to its junction with the spinal cord. From this lowly location, about half a million serotonin-producing nerve cells of the human brain send long, branching projections up into the cerebral hemispheres where they make synaptic connections with hundreds of millions of other nerve cells. These evolutionary and anatomical facts have significant implications. They tell us that serotonin is likely to be important for rather basic functions of the nervous system, like the regulation of sleep and eating; otherwise why would the human serotonin system look like a scaled-up version of the worm's serotonin system? But knowing that serotonin is normally important for brain functions that are disordered in depression is not the same thing as knowing that serotonin deficiency is the cause of depression. To make that claim stand up on its own two feet we need data from depressed patients to show that they have low levels of serotonin in their brains. And this crucial piece of evidence for the serotonin theory of depression has never really materialised, despite decades of searching for it.

I found this out most acutely that day in the outpatient clinic at the Maudsley Hospital when I was assuring a patient that SSRIs would rebalance the level of serotonin in his brain. "How do you know that about me," he asked, "how do you know that the level of serotonin is imbalanced in my brain?" We both immediately knew that I didn't have an answer to that question. I didn't even have a clue about how to find out the answer. After this silent moment of truth, we politely carried on in the customary way. He left with a prescription for an SSRI and an appointment to return in six weeks to tell me if it had made any difference. He left me feeling like a total fraud. For the first time in my medical career, I had seen myself as if performing the farcical role of one of Molière's ludicrous "leeches", a vacuous 17th-century physician, telling patients they needed to be bled because of their superfluous sanguinity, without really knowing how much blood they had or how much they needed.

Bereft of biomarkers

Which brings me finally to what I now think is the simplest way of saying why it all went wrong after Prozac: no biomarkers.

In most areas of medicine, doctors are using biomarkers all the time. A biomarker is just a measurement of a biological function or a biochemical in patients. Haemoglobin is a bread-and-butter biomarker, easily measurable by a blood test, that can be used to diagnose anaemia, or too few red cells in the blood. Haemoglobin can also be used to predict the response of an anaemic patient to treatment with a blood transfusion, or to identify the much rarer patients with too many red cells in circulation, who might actually benefit from a bleeding operation as prescribed by one of Molière's physicians. Haemoglobin is thus, in technical parlance, both a diagnostic and a predictive biomarker. Glucose is another familiar example of a biomarker that is both diagnostic, of diabetes mellitus, and predictive, of therapeutic response to insulin. There are already hundreds of thousands of biomarkers, and they are rapidly growing in number and sophistication, in all areas of medicine... except psychiatry, which doesn't currently have a single blood test or biomarker to its name.[39]

In a rational universe, the use of SSRIs, and the serotonin theory of depression, would be informed and justified by serotonin biomarkers. When a patient came to see me for advice about how to treat his depression, I would measure the serotonin level in his brain and, if this level was low, I would recommend a drug that was likely to increase serotonin. We could repeat the brain biomarker measurement a few weeks after start of treatment, to check that serotonin levels were returning to normal. Serotonin biomarkers would allow us to use SSRIs without wishful thinking or farcical hand-waving, and much to the benefit of patients. But serotonin biomarkers have never materialised in clinical practice and they are very challenging to measure even in a specialised research study.

The fundamental difficulty in measuring serotonin bio-markers relates to the anatomy of the serotonin system. There aren't very many serotonin-manufacturing nerve cells in the human brain and they're mostly concentrated in a few small clusters in the brain stem. The only conceivable way of measuring the level of serotonin in these cells, in a living human, is by brain scanning or neuroimaging. And in practice it is very difficult to make any kind of image of such a small and inaccessible part of the brain. Some studies have used special scanners to measure levels of serotonin transporters in patients with depression.[40] But the requisite technology is expensive, difficult to use outside a few specialist centres, and involves the patient receiving a small but significant dose of a radioactively labelled drug. It could never be used as a biomarker in everyday clinical practice and it has not been much used as such in research studies of depression and serotonin.

The only other options are to measure serotonin and related

molecules in the blood; or in the cerebrospinal fluid (CSF), the watery liquid that flows through the internal chambers or ventricles of the brain. Both options have been explored in research studies but not pursued into practice. Blood biomarkers of serotonin have not been reliably diagnostic of depression, or predictive of response to SSRIs, and are probably not very representative of serotonin levels in the brain. CSF biomarkers are more likely to be representative of brain serotonin levels than blood biomarkers. But taking a CSF sample for molecular analysis requires a lumbar puncture or spinal tap: inserting a long needle between two verte-brae at the base of the spine, and withdrawing a couple of teaspoons of fluid. The extra diagnostic gain from CSF sero-tonin biomarkers has not justified the extra pain of lumbar punctures.

So it is not for want of trying that we don't have biomarkers to guide serotonin-tweaking drug treatments for depression. But we don't. And in the absence of biomarkers, we will never have a straight answer for patients about why they should take SSRIs. We will continue to proceed by trial and error, trying one drug then another if the first one doesn't work. Perhaps most regrettably, we will be encouraged to behave as if all depression were the same. If we can't tell the difference between the depressed patients with high serotonin levels and those with low serotonin levels, then we will often assume, as I did in the Maudsley Hospital outpatient clinic, that they must all have low serotonin levels, they must all be the same, to justify prescribing the same first-line treatment for everyone with depression.

Yet when we say they are all the same, or when we don't say

it out loud but we act as if it was the case, that all depressed people are depressed for the same reason and they are all likely to benefit from the same treatment, we should stop and think about what we mean by the word "they". In this context, it represents about 10% of the global population at any one time, or about 25% of everyone over the course of their lifetimes, or at least one member of all the families on the planet. I would dare to say that none of us will live our lives untouched by depression, directly or indirectly. So there isn't really much difference between "them" and "us", when it comes to depression, although the culture of stigmatisation would have you believe otherwise. And, for me at least, it beggars belief that such a huge chunk of humanity should suffer from the oscillations of a single unmeasurable molecule in the brain. The serotonin theory in that sense is as unsatisfactory as the Freudian theory of unquantifiable libido or the Hippocratic theory of non-existent black bile.

⟶▸▣◉ ◉▣◂⟵

In short, depression after Descartes is in a sorry state. According to the prevailing dualist orthodoxy that he bequeathed us, it is officially a disorder of the mind, and as such it may be exacerbated by stigmatisation, or alleviated by psychotherapy. But it is also treated unofficially as if it was a disorder of the brain, using drugs for which we lack a rationale beyond the reach of satire. We deal with depression as if it is not entirely of the mind but not truly part of the brain or body either. We don't agree with each other about how to deal with it better – there is grumbling contention, a culture war, a bit of name calling, between psychologically minded advocates of a more "brainless" approach, on the one hand, and neuroscience-driven advocates of a more "mindless" approach, on the other. Meanwhile, we have had no major new treatments for a generation and the limitations of the existing drugs and talking therapies are obvious. Despite increasing access to psychotherapy, despite increasing numbers of prescriptions for SSRIs at decreasing cost per pill, depression is still expected to be the single biggest cause of disability in the world by 2030. It is not cancer, or heart disease, or rheumatoid arthritis, or TB, or any other physical disease, that accounts for economic costs in the order of 3% of GDP in rich countries. It is mental health disorders, principally depression. And we don't really know what to say or do about it.

It's time to turn the page.

Chapter 5

HOW?

Extraordinary claims demand extraordinary evidence

Around the time of Prozac's launch, circa 1990, as the wave of therapeutic excitement triggered by the accidental anti-depressant discoveries of the 1950s was peaking, a few papers were obscurely published. They had titles like "Stress and immunity: an integrated view of relationships between the brain and the immune system" (1989);[41] "The macrophage theory of depression" (1991);[5] "Evidence for an immune response in major depression" (1995).[6] These and related papers were necessarily published in obscure journals because their scientific hypothesis could hardly have been more transgressive, more ideologically scandalous – in a word, flakier. They proposed that mood states were somehow related to the activity of white blood cells, that the mind was connected to the body across the Cartesian divide. In the scientific climate of the time, this idea was not even wrong. It was worse than that. It was tantamount to proposing that mood states were related to the flow of black bile and other occult humours. And, quite properly, for many years this theory was either ignored or attended to only with a high degree of scepticism by most other scientists.

It is often difficult to pinpoint historically when a new scientific theory breaks through. We all stand on each other's shoulders, almost all new ideas are incrementally derived from older ideas, and the book of knowledge grows gradually, as a result of the collective efforts of many individual scientists working on the same page. It is even more difficult to recognise a breakthrough at the time it is happening, rather than retrospectively, because, by definition, a breakthrough breaks things. It must disrupt or unsettle or undermine or challenge some prior certainty. So, at the moment of its insurgency, a scientific breakthrough will be resisted, denied, obscured or ridiculed by all right-minded supporters of the status quo.

Those early papers in neuro-immunology or immuno-psychiatry now look like a breakthrough to me. Their shared idea – that mood and inflammation are linked – was a scientific reformulation of what is common knowledge among patients, if not among their physicians. We all know that mood disorders are closely associated with physical disorders. All of us have had occasional experiences of fatigue, social withdrawal, low mood and other depressive symptoms after a physical injury, like a bone fracture or dental surgery, a chest infection or a vaccination. It seems obvious to many non-medical people that physical and mental health are closely linked. The innovative idea of immuno-psychiatry is that this association is explained by the immune system. And to test this idea, scientists conducted the first experiments to measure biomarkers of inflammation – white blood cells and cytokines – in depressed patients.

This was unprecedented: it was the first time that we began to apply the power and precision of modern immunology to help us understand human behaviour and depression. And for at least 15 years this seminal endeavour was conventionally regarded as beyond the pale. In 2012, when I caught up with the story, when I first began to see how there might be something in it, that immunological mechanisms might cause depression, and that anti-inflammatory drugs might even be a new type of anti-depressant, I consulted senior colleagues, as you do.

"I'd always thought you were more sensible than that," said the Regius Professor of Physic in the University of Cambridge (who was sort of joking). "If you'd come to me with this idea five years ago, I'd have thought you were crazy; but now I'm not so sure," said the Senior Vice President of R&D in GlaxoSmithKline (who wasn't joking).

You won't be surprised that I think the core assumption of Cartesian dualism – the conventional idea that mind and body are distinct domains – lies deep beneath this scepticism. But if you scratch the surface of their resistance to neuro-immunology or immuno-psychiatry, sophisticated scientists these days won't invoke Descartes by name (they mostly think philosophy is irrelevant to the day job). Instead they will ask about evidence, causality and mechanism. They want to get to the crux of the matter.

Scientists want to be convinced that there really is a causal relationship between inflammation and depression. Then they want to know how and why.

How, exactly, step by step, can inflammatory changes in the body's immune system cause changes in the way the brain works so as to make people feel depressed?

Why is the depressed patient inflamed in the first place? And why should the body's inflammatory response, which is supposed to be on our side, which has evolved to help us win the battle against disease, be causing us to feel depressed?

It is a big ask. But it is not an unreasonable ask, or too high a price to pay for scientific credibility. Extraordinary claims demand extraordinary evidence and, in a Cartesian world, what could be more extraordinary than the body being linked to the mind through the immune system?

A stubborn fact

Many of the first immuno-psychiatrists used the same simple, experimental design to get started on their pioneering endeavour. They recruited two groups of volunteers, a group of patients with major depressive disorder, or MDD (called the cases), and a group of healthy people (called the controls). They collected a sample of blood from each volunteer and measured a few inflammatory biomarkers in the blood: either cytokines or C-reactive protein (CRP), which is produced by the liver in response to high levels of cytokines and is therefore useful as an indirect marker of the body's state of inflammation. Then these biomarker data were analysed to estimate the size of the difference between cases and controls, and to test the probability that the difference was statistically significant, meaning it was unlikely to have occurred by chance.

In the 20-plus years between 1992 and 2014, immuno-psychiatrists have reported cytokine measurements on thousands of MDD cases and healthy controls.[42] Collectively, these data show that the blood concentrations of CRP and some cytokines are increased in patients with depression. The probability of seeing differences this big by chance is in the order of one in 10,000.

It's not a massive effect but it's there:[43] on average, people with depression have moderately but significantly increased blood cytokine levels compared to non-depressed people.

These case-control studies, which measure levels of an inflammatory biomarker like CRP in depressed cases compared to healthy controls, start from the idea that it is reasonable to put people into one of two categorically distinct boxes – depressed or healthy. A case-control comparison formalises the common assumption that depression can be conceived in terms of us and them: we are perfectly healthy and they are very different from us because they are depressed. But there is another way of looking at things, which starts from the idea that we are all on a spectrum, we all have some experience of depressive symptoms, mild or severe, and in real life there is not a black-and-white distinction between depressed cases and healthy controls. Taking this more dimensional approach, the question is whether people who are located towards the more severe end of the depressive spectrum tend to have higher blood levels of inflammatory markers; and the answer is yes, they do.

One of the largest studies to date measured CRP and depressive symptoms in 73,131 people recruited from the population of Copenhagen.[44] Ordinary members of the Danish general public who frequently experienced low-grade depressive symptoms – such as thinking that they weren't accomplishing much or wanting to give up – had significantly higher blood CRP levels than those who didn't. There was something like a dose–response relationship in the data: the higher the dose of inflammation indicated by CRP, the greater the depressive response in terms of negatively biased, self-critical thoughts. The probability that this relationship could have occurred by chance was reckoned to be less than one in a trillion.

This is an impressively solid piece of evidence to add to the cumulative evidence from case-control studies of MDD. We now know that people feeling somewhat depressed in the course of their ordinary lives, as well as the more severely affected patients, are more likely to be inflamed. It is important to be clear that these studies don't prove that everyone with depression is inflamed; or that everyone who is inflamed will be depressed. But they do give us very robust statistical evidence that depression and inflammation occur together much more often than we would expect as a result of random coincidence or bad luck. And as the studies have accumulated since the pioneering work of the 1990s, the evidence has become progressively more solid. Depression is associated with biomarker evidence of bodily inflammation. It's the stubborn survival of a disruptive fact. But this result alone does not prove that the relationship between inflammation and depression is causal. We need to get a tighter grip on the slippery but crucial issue of causality to begin to answer the how question.

Causes must come first

We know, by definition, that effects follow causes or that causes precede effects. So, if inflammation caused depression, we would expect that people were inflamed before they became depressed. Many of us will have had personal experiences of feeling low, blue, depressed, subdued or tearful after (not before) an infectious illness or some other inflammatory episode. My experience of post-dental melancholia was certainly consistent with the ordering of inflammation before depression in time: I felt fine before I went to the dentist and suffered a cytokine squall; then I felt lethargic, isolated and pessimistic for the following 24 hours.

One way to study the sequencing of inflammation and depression is by making repeated measurements of cytokine levels and mood states in the same people followed up repeatedly over a period of time. The 2014 study of 15,000 children born in south-west England, which followed them up repeatedly from nine to 18 years old, found that cytokine levels at the age of nine predicted the risk of depression at the age of 18.[7] The children who had blood cytokine levels in the top third of the range aged nine were about one-and-a-half times more likely to become depressed aged 18 than the children who had lower levels as nine-year-olds. Importantly, the children with higher cytokine levels were no more depressed than their less inflamed contemporaries when they were first assessed at the age of nine. They only became depressed after they were inflamed.

Similar results emerged from another study, towards the other end of the life cycle, of UK civil servants working in Whitehall.[45] About 2,000 people in their sixties were assessed for mood and inflammation on three occasions, in 2004, 2008 and 2012. Low-grade inflammation was quite common in this group of older people. Four hundred of them were chronically inflamed, with high CRP levels in both 2004 and 2008, but were not depressed at the time of these first two assessments. However, their risk of becoming depressed for the first time in 2012 was significantly increased, especially if they were women. A woman with high CRP levels in 2004 and 2008 was about three times more likely to become depressed for the first time in 2012 than a woman with no CRP evidence of inflammation previously.

These long-term follow-up studies, in two very different age groups, demonstrate that increased inflammation can precede depression. But still these results alone are not sufficient to establish a causal mechanism. To put it another way, if inflammation at the age of nine did *not* increase the risk of depression at the age of 18, a sceptic might reasonably conclude that a causal influence of depression had been ruled out or refuted. However, the opposite result, as was actually observed, is not so decisively affirmative. Showing that cytokine levels in the blood predict scores on a depression questionnaire four or nine years later is permissive of a causal role for inflammation; but not by itself conclusive or compelling. The time interval between inflammatory cause and depressive effect is too long, and the underlying chain of events that presumably sustains the causal process over many years is tenuously understood. However, we can begin to close that explanatory gap by looking at the relationship between inflammation and depression over much shorter periods of time.

One of the many areas of medicine where immunology has delivered therapeutic progress in my lifetime is treatment for hepatitis. This is a viral infection that comes in three forms, A, B and C. Hepatitis B is particularly dangerous because the virus can lurk within liver cells for many years, evading the immune system's routine efforts to eliminate it completely, causing chronic inflammation and scarring of the liver (also known as cirrhosis), and increasing the risk of cancer of the liver. Among the first treatments to make a difference to this dismal prognosis was interferon, an inflammatory cytokine. The therapeutic rationale is that the hepatitis B virus is immunologically camouflaged; the patient's immune system doesn't naturally see it as the mortal threat it is, and so his immune response must be massively boosted to help him clear the virus completely.

Since the stakes are so high it has been ethically acceptable for an effective treatment to be extremely unpleasant, which interferon is. All patients immediately react to it as if it was a severe infection – they become feverish, lethargic and anorexic – the same cluster of symptoms, called sickness behaviour, that you'd expect to see in a rat injected with cytokines. This is not a side effect but a sign that the treatment is having its intended, principal effect of stimulating an inflammatory response. Over a few weeks, most patients recover from the acute effects of interferon treatment but about a third become clinically depressed. They are persistently lethargic and anorexic, self-critical, guilty and pessimistic, as well as anhedonic or lacking a sense of pleasure,[46] the opposite of pleasure-seeking hedonists.

It is important to be clear that this happens to people who were not depressed immediately before the interferon injection. Their experience provides some of the clearest evidence in humans that an inflammatory stimulus can cause depression. By comparing the patients that become depressed following interferon to those that don't, we can understand something more about the mechanisms involved. It turns out that patients with a background history of depression are more likely to become depressed again following interferon. This could be because they have a genetic predisposition to respond depressively to inflammation. And indeed there is some evidence that people with a genetic profile that makes them more likely to get inflamed, to produce high levels of cytokines, are more likely to become depressed after interferon treatment.[47]

Putting it all together, from the long-term epidemiological follow-up studies, to the experiences of patients following interferon treatment, and even including my anecdote about root canal blues, there is evidence that bodily inflammation can precede depression. And if inflammation occurs before depression then it could cause depression. We haven't yet answered the question how. But we have at least established that it is a question worth asking in more biological detail.

The Berlin wall in the brain

I was not always a happy medical student in the first half of the 1980s. I did my clinical training at St Bartholomew's Hospital in the City of London, which was founded in 1123 outside the city walls by Rahere, a monk and a minstrel in the court of Henry I. Henry VIII refounded the hospital in the 16th century; Harvey did his experiments there on the circulation of the blood in the 17th century; Hogarth painted the murals in its Great Hall in the 18th century; and, in 1878, according to Conan Doyle, Dr Watson met Sherlock Holmes for the first time in a chemistry lab at Bart's, where Holmes, perhaps blazing the trail that Freud would later follow, was investigating the pharmacological properties of a "little pinch of the latest vegetable alkaloid".[48]

Bart's had long been home to some of the most eminent medical minds in London. Percival Pott, to name but one, was an 18th-century surgeon who had the unrivalled honour of two diseases named after him in our textbooks: tuberculosis (TB) of the spine and the chimney-sweep's disease of cancer of the scrotum. Pott worked out that scrotal cancer was caused by exposure to carcinogens in chimney soot and he led legislation that banned the practice of sending orphan boys as young as five or six climbing up chimneys to clean them. Bart's proudly claimed him as the first doctor in history to find a cause and a cure for a cancer. The hospital had been there for all of London's plagues, from the Black Death in the Middle Ages to TB in the Victorian era; it had survived all of London's disasters, from the Great Fire to the Blitz. It was an ancient, enduring and honourable institution.

However, perhaps for that very reason, the way that Bart's taught medicine at the time was by a dogmatic and didactic apprenticeship: motto, you can always tell a Bart's man but you can't tell him much. We had to learn endless lists of symptoms, signs and pathophysiological catechisms – like the 32 causes of anaemia – and were often quizzed by consultants on teaching rounds to recite these lists in front of other students and staff. It was important under the stress of this ritualised public interrogation not to blurt out wrong answers or, almost as bad, the right answers but in the wrong order.

"A woman comes to see you with a headache, what are the first 10 diagnostic tests you'd do?" If your immediate response was "A brain scan" that deserved some supplementary sarcasm because, as any fule kno,[49] that wasn't the first thing, it was more like the 10th thing, you'd do. "What's the first thing you'd do?" "Talk to the patient." "Thank you. And what are the first three questions you'd ask her?"

And so it went on in the time-honoured fashion for three years. We were being drilled as much as trained, over-learning or hard-wiring certain key nuggets of medical knowledge, and learning by example a certain style, and language, and way of working as a doctor. We were generally not encouraged to question too much of the wisdom of senior physicians and surgeons. I was not the only student to resent being taught like this and almost all of us got through it OK. But I think it explains the great pleasure it gives me now to see false facts, which I was taught to learn with black-and-white certainty, on pain of public humiliation, being scientifically usurped by new knowledge (Fig. 9).

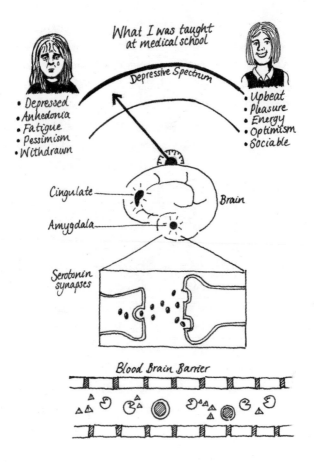

Figure 9: What I was taught at medical school, in the 1980s (left) was that depression was caused by reduced levels of serotonin in synapses between nerve cells. It was also common knowledge that the brain was completely separated from the body's immune system by the blood–brain barrier (BBB), a wall of densely packed endothelial cells, which did not allow circulating macrophages or cytokines to enter the brain.

What we know now (right) is that there are many channels of communication across the BBB. Inflammation of the body can cause activation of the inflammatory microglial cells in the brain, which

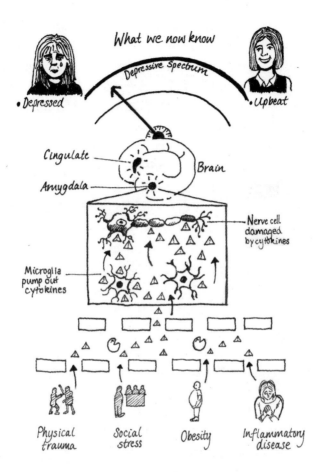

in turn causes collateral damage to nerve cells in the amygdala, the cingulate and other hubs in the brain's emotional network. We can also see more clearly that there are many potentially relevant drivers of inflammation. Auto-immune disease, like Mrs P's arthritis, obesity and physical trauma can all cause bodily inflammation. But so too can social stress, even a brief and relatively mild stress like public speaking. It used to be impossible to imagine that inflammation and depression were mechanistically connected; now we are getting closer to answers to the questions of how and why inflammation could cause depression.

The brain is immune privileged – that is what we were taught at medical school not all that long ago. It sits behind the blood–brain barrier (BBB) and the cells and cytokines of the immune system simply can't get at it. The BBB rigidly defended the brain from the inflammatory storms of the body. It could only be breached by the immune system in the wake of catastrophic damage to the brain, such as the surprise attack of a stroke or the remorseless growth of a tumour. Under more normal operating conditions, the BBB was assumed to be an impermeable defence of the brain's unique privilege to work beyond the reach of the immune system. To the extent that this dogma was true, it would obviously be a major obstacle in the mechanistic path from an inflammatory protein in the blood to a state of mind. If peripheral inflammatory signals can't get across the BBB, they can't have any effects on the brain; and if they can't have effects on the brain, then how can they have effects on mood or behaviour? You can see why the Berlin version of the BBB was one of the most concrete formulations of Cartesian dualism. It enforced segregation of the inflamed body and the mind by blocking any communication between them. Happily, it's mostly wrong.

Even at the time, the analogy wasn't exact. The Berlin wall was built from slabs of reinforced concrete whereas the BBB, we were told, was built from millions of cellular bricks, the endothelial cells, that formed the inner lining of the blood vessels in the brain and were very tightly connected to each other. There was literally no space for immune cells, or even large molecules like cytokines, to get between the endothelial cells, as they would have to do if they were to migrate from the bloodstream into the brain tissue on the other side of the barrier. To turn the analogy around, it was as if the Berlin wall was supposed to be impenetrable mainly because it was built out of bricks that were held together by an especially dense, adhesive mortar.

Now we know that there are some parts of the brain where this is simply not the case: there are gaps between adjacent endothelial cells – there are chinks in the mortar – that are big enough to allow big molecules, like proteins, to diffuse freely from the blood into the brain. More radically, it turns out that the endothelial bricks in the wall are not inert, like bricks of baked clay; they are double agents in the immune system's communications network. One side of each cell forms the inner lining of a blood vessel – an artery or vein – and the other side of the cell forms the outer surface of the vessel, in close proximity to nerve cells and microglial cells (the brain's robocops). The inner surfaces of the endothelial barrier are covered with cytokine receptors, so they can detect inflammatory signals communicated by cytokines circulating in the blood. Endothelial cells can then relay these inflammatory signals into the brain and activate the brain's resident macrophages, so that the brain becomes inflamed in response to inflammation in the rest of the body.

The "wall" is not only permeable to inflammatory proteins, it is also permeable to the much larger inflammatory cells that are continually circulating through the cardiovascular system. The inner surface of the wall can make itself attractive to circulating white blood cells and actively assist their passage into the brain, squeezing through specially created gaps between endothelial "bricks". It was even discovered a few years ago that the brain has a system of lymphatic vessels that drain immune cells and proteins from it into nearby lymph nodes, where they can mingle with other cells of the immune system and then return to the blood circulation.[50] In direct contradiction to what we were taught as certain knowledge in the 1980s, the brain is not cut off from the immune system in the body. There is free and easy communication by many channels in both directions across the BBB.[51]

My personal favourite of these many freshly discovered modes of communication between the brain and the body is called the inflammatory reflex.[52] We have known since Freud's old friend was working on the Hering-Breuer reflex that the vagus nerve controls the heart rate, causing it to decrease when the lungs are fully inflated. As medical students, we were taught that the Hering-Breuer reflex was one among many reflexes that allowed the brain automatically to monitor and control numerous bodily functions including blood pressure, sweating, stomach acid and the rhythmic contractions of the gut. At the time it never occurred to me to wonder if the same kind of reflex might also allow the brain automatically to monitor and control the inflammatory state of the body. But in the last decade or so it has been discovered that there is indeed such an inflammatory reflex, mediated by the vagus nerve (Fig. 10).

Reflexes are circuits in the nervous system that automatically link an incoming stimulus to a predetermined response. In the inflammatory reflex circuit, the input stimulus is the level of inflammatory cytokines in the blood. The sensory fibres of the vagus nerve have cytokine receptors on their surface, so if cytokine levels increase in the body, the vagus nerve will detect this change in inflammatory status, and send

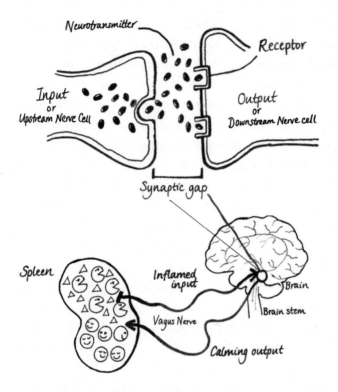

Figure 10: Nervous reflex control of inflammation. The vagus nerve detects high levels of inflammatory cytokines produced by angry macrophages in the spleen and sends an inflamed input signal to the brain. In the brain, the nerve cells carrying the input signal make synaptic connections with output nerve cells that carry a calming, anti-inflammatory signal from the brain back to the spleen.

an electrical signal straight across the BBB direct to the brain. This will immediately trigger an output signal to leave the brain, crossing the BBB in the opposite direction, travelling through the motor fibres of the vagus, to reach the spleen, which is one of the major command-and-control centres of the immune system, stuffed full of white blood cells. The nerve fibres of the vagus are finely branched throughout the spleen, coming into close contact with millions of immune cells, and the vagal signal makes macrophages become less angry, less activated and less productive of cytokines. In short, the vagus picks up a high cytokine signal in the body and reflexively acts on macrophages in the spleen so that cytokine levels fall (Fig. 10).

This is an example of the general principle of homeostasis by negative feedback. The vagus is acting homeostatically – literally, to keep things the same – by having an inhibitory effect – or feeding back negatively – on macrophages that would otherwise produce an excessive quantity of cytokines. The inflammatory reflex is one of those discoveries that makes me think both "how surprising" and "how obvious" – once it has been made. It is another example of the vagus nerve doing what the vagus generally does – which is to calm things down in the body. In the perfect light of hindsight, it is just what you'd expect physiologically. But it could have some interesting implications therapeutically.

The idea of stimulating the vagus nerve for symptom relief has been around for a long time, dating back at least as far as the alderman's itch. The story was told at Bart's that high officials of the medieval city of London and its guilds – the aldermen – were martyrs to the indigestion they suffered as a result of feasting at great banquets. They couldn't rise from the table before the Mayor; so they had to deal with their dyspeptic symptoms discreetly and while remaining seated. They found a way to do this by massaging the auricle, the flexible collagen ridge in their shell-like outer ears, just above the opening that lets sound pass through to the inner ear. Rubbing your auricle is good first aid for indigestion and anxiety: that's the alderman's itch.

The reason it works, which the Bart's physicians assumed was unknown to the ignorant aldermen, is that the small patch of skin over the auricle is the only point on the body surface where the sense of touch is mediated by the vagus. Rubbing the skin of the auricle stimulates the vagus's sensory fibres and sends a signal to the brain; this triggers a reflex response through a different branch of the vagus to the stomach, making it reduce its production of irritating gastric acid, the cause of most dyspeptic symptoms.

You could try it the next time you want to make your stomach less acidic. Don't expect miracles – but it can be better than nothing. If you're disappointed by the stomach-calming effects of simply massaging one auricle at a time, you can try rubbing both of them, while simultaneously taking a deep breath and holding it. Then you will be stimulating your vagus nerve in two ways – by the alderman's itch and the Hering-Breuer reflex. This would be a socially challenging technique to use under the radar at the Lord Mayor's banquet but, as I was taught as a child, it is an excellent cure for hiccups.

Now there are many other ways of stimulating the vagus nerve than by the alderman's itch. There are vibrating devices that sit in the ear like a hearing aid and rub your auricle for you. More invasively, it is also possible to implant electrical stimulators in the body that can deliver a precisely timed sequence of shocks to the vagus nerve. This requires a surgical procedure but it is not a difficult operation. The fibres of the vagus nerve are surgically accessible as they travel south from the brain stem to the abdomen and the spleen. Electrodes can be applied to the nerve directly, and the nerve can then be electrically stimulated under the control of the patient or the physician.

Since increased signalling by the vagus nerve inhibits cytokine production by macrophages in the spleen, it is predictable that electrically stimulating the vagus nerve should reduce cytokine levels in patients with inflammatory disease. When this procedure was recently tested in patients with rheumatoid arthritis, the results were as predicted but nonetheless startling.[53] Electrical stimulation of the vagus nerve for 20 minutes per day caused rapid and substantial reductions in blood cytokine levels and the patients reported fewer painful joint symptoms. When the stimulation was experimentally stopped for 10 days, both cytokine levels and symptom scores increased; when the stimulation was reinstated, cytokines and symptoms both obediently decreased again. By stimulating (or not stimulating) the vagus nerve, we can turn off (or turn on) bodily inflammation in rheumatoid arthritis, literally at the flick of a switch. It's a wonderfully disruptive discovery, based on science that didn't exist when I was a lad, and it opens up a whole new field of bio-electronic medicine, using electronic stimulators to control or restore the immune system.

Inflamed brains

Since I left medical school, in 1985, the wall in Berlin and the wall in the brain have both been destroyed. We now know that the BBB is open for communication, in many different ways, between the immune system and the nervous system. The BBB does not enforce a hard Cartesian divide between brain and body and it no longer stands in the way of a mechanistic explanation of how inflammation might cause depression. It is important to know that a cytokine signal in the blood can get across the BBB; it is an important step forward in the direction of knowing how. But to answer the how question completely, we still need to understand what an inflammatory signal could do to the brain, once it gets there, that would make people more likely to feel depressed.

The most practical way to get at this question in humans is by using brain-scanning technologies, like functional magnetic resonance imaging. Using fMRI, we can scan the human brain for changes in blood flow while people are looking at different things, or doing different tasks. The parts of the brain that are most important for doing a particular task, or perceiving a particular stimulus, have the greatest increases in blood flow and will appear as hotspots on an fMRI brain scan. How can we use this technology to investigate an emotional state, like sadness or depression?

As Charles Darwin recognised, more than 100 years before the first fMRI scanners were invented, we are highly evolved to detect emotional expressions in the faces of other people. And when I see a face that is expressing a particular emotion, the sight of it will induce that same emotion in me. So if I want to make people feel sad during an fMRI experiment, then I can simply show them pictures of sad faces while they are lying in the scanner. This experiment has been done hundreds of times and the results are pretty consistent. Seeing sad faces, and experiencing a slight sense of sadness as a result, reliably causes increased blood flow to four or five parts of the human brain, with esoteric names like the amygdala and the cingulate cortex (Fig. 9). The brain regions that are activated by sadness and other emotions in humans are synaptically connected to each other and we can think of them collectively as an emotional brain network. This is the nervous infrastructure that underpins our subjective emotional states, our moments of grief, sorrow and sadness. Although it enables something very personal to each of us, our feelings and moods, this infrastructure is not unique to any of us. It is shared between humans, of course, but also with other animals. Darwin didn't know any of this but he would not have been surprised to learn that some of the components of the human emotional brain network, like the amygdala, go back as far as the reptiles in evolutionary time.

One of the things that fMRI has shown us about depression is that it is often linked to changes in this pre-human emotional brain network. When depressed people look at a sad face, they activate their sadness-generating brain networks in the same way as healthy people, but more so.[54] MDD has been consistently associated with over-activation of the amygdala and the cingulate,[55] whereas depressed patients who became less depressed over the course of several weeks of treatment with a selective serotonin reuptake inhibitor (SSRI) had significantly reduced activation of the amygdala.[56] In short, we now have a much better idea, than we did before the advent of fMRI, about how the mental states of depression are linked to changes in brain function. Knowing this, we'd expect that inflammatory signals or shocks from the body, which are now known to cause depressive symptoms, should increase activation of the emotional brain network. How can we test this idea safely in humans?

Vaccination is a good example of a safe inflammatory shock that transiently causes a depressive state. Vaccination must produce a protective immune response if it is to be effective in preventing infection in the medium term; but in the short term it also often causes mood and behavioural changes. The last time I was vaccinated, with a cocktail of typhoid, tetanus and hepatitis vaccines, the nurse warned me in a matter-of-fact way that I would probably feel a bit "off colour" for a few days and might even need to take a day off work. She didn't tell me why. When I asked her why, she didn't really have an answer: "It's just your body's way of dealing with it." But even though she couldn't explain it, she could predict it. She was right, I did feel a bit off colour for 24 hours or so. It was not too bad compared to the impact of root canal surgery but I was tired and irritable that evening, complaining miserably to my family that we were all sure to die of bilharzia or malaria, or some other tropical disease that you can't be vaccinated against, on our upcoming once-in-a-lifetime African holiday. So you'd predict that if I had been scanned a day after my vaccination, when I was finding it so hard to feel pleasure, my emotional brain hotspots would have been hotter than they were the day before, when I was feeling fine.

This prediction was recently put to the test, when 20 healthy young people had fMRI scanning done twice while they looked at pictures of emotional faces, once after a typhoid vaccination and once after a placebo injection.[8] The vaccination increased levels of cytokines in the blood and caused mild depressive symptoms. It also caused an increase in activity of the cingulate cortex that was associated with the severity of depressive symptoms, such that the people who were most depressed by the vaccination, and the people who had the strongest inflammatory cytokine response to vaccination, showed the greatest changes in emotional brain network connectivity. The brain's "way of dealing with it" is a bit more complicated than they made it sound in the travel clinic, but scientifically it makes sense that the inflammatory shock of vaccination causes increased activation of emotional brain hotspots, which in turn, causes mild depressive symptoms for a few days after the jab.

fMRI is a marvellous technology and we are lucky to have it. But it will never be able to completely explain the mechanisms by which inflammation causes depression. This is because the smallest thing an fMRI scanner can see in the human brain is approximately one cubic millimetre. That is about the size of the legendary pinhead. It is a technological tour de force that we can measure such a small volume of human brain tissue, painlessly, affordably, almost risklessly, and in about 15 minutes. However, the spatial resolution of fMRI is nowhere near good enough (and never will be) to see individual cells or neurons. A single cubic millimetre contains about 100,000 nerve cells. And to understand the effects of inflammation on the brain more completely, to take the next big step in the direction of how, we need to know what's going on at the level of nerve cells and microglial cells.

To get down to that level of detail, we need to change the focus of scientific investigation from humans to other species, like rats and mice, or to cells cultured or grown in test tubes. This would give us the advantage of much better spatial resolution, and a much tighter experimental grip on precisely detailed questions about the mechanisms by which immune cells can change the way nerve cells work. However, the scientific value of animal experiments in depression is often taxed by the challenge of translating this finer-grained biological science in "lower" animals to the understanding and treatment of depressive disorders in humans.

Translation from animal neuroscience to the human condition has been problematic since Descartes, who did not credit animals with souls. The most exalted states of mind, such as communion with God, were therefore not supposed to exist in animals. But of course Descartes recognised that animals often behaved intelligently or adaptively in response to the world around them. So he proposed that some functions of the mind – like memory and emotion – could be mechanistically delivered by the physical machinery of the brain alone. This was in contrast to the "higher", more distinctively human aspects of consciousness, like a sense of beauty or truth, which depended on mysterious infusions of volatile animal spirits from the heart-heated blood to the pineal gland.

The question for Descartes, and for us as his philosophical heirs, is where do you draw the line? How do you divide the human condition overall into a piece that is explicable by the brain machine, as it is in animals, and a piece that is inexplicable in the language of the world, and only known to us subjectively, as human beings? As he reflected on this question, Descartes became progressively more inclined to the view that a lot of the human condition was animal-like. By his untimely end, he regarded only the most spiritually, aesthetically or intellectually intense ideas as distinctively human. The vast majority of human life, almost everything else going on in the world outside him, all the routine business of feeding, sleeping, mating, parenting, competing and collaborating, all that normal life-living stuff that people do, he could conceive was not especially human. Most of the human condition could be engineered by the human brain machine in much the same way as similar behaviours must be engineered by the brain machine in dogs or cats, since they have no animating souls.

Thus Descartes might have been gung-ho about the value of modern animal experiments to understand more about the human disorder of depression. He might have reasoned that since depression affects sleep, appetite, sociability, physical activity – all of which are forms of animal behaviour – those symptoms at least should be driven purely by brain machinery in humans, and so could be usefully informed by experiments on animals. On the other hand, he might have worried, what about the dark, guilty visions and the spiritual or existential torments of the melancholic mind? What about the conviction that one is personally worthless? Or the certain knowledge that one's future can only be grim? These must be exclusively human experiences, which could not be informed in any way by an animal experiment, and yet may be the most profoundly shattering symptoms of mood disorder. In which case, Descartes might muse, it is hard to see the point of using animals in mental health research.

This doubt continues to run through all animal research in psychiatry and psychology. I have found that a good Cartesian doctor can feel perfectly entitled to dismiss the whole field out of hand. "Nobody believes animal models in psychiatry," I have been told several times with great authority. And then, at least once, as if the whole thing was an anthropomorphic pantomime: "Next you'll be telling me that rats can feel sorry for themselves, or that mice sometimes wonder if life's worth living!"

But seriously, I think, it is the gung-ho side of Descartes' position that has been more clearly vindicated by animal research into how inflammation can cause depressive behaviours. As we saw in chapter 1, it has been established that when a rat or a mouse is inflamed, its behaviour immediately and profoundly changes in a complex but predictable way. The inflamed rat becomes less active, it eats and drinks less, it shuns the company of other rats, and its sleep/wake cycle is disturbed. It shows sickness behaviours. Following a single, acute inflammatory shock – like an injection of lipopolysaccharide (LPS), the molecular barcode that makes macrophages see red – the rat's behaviour changes almost immediately and remains highly abnormal for 24-48 hours, before gradually returning to normal over the course of several days. If it then has a second dose of LPS this will again be followed by days of sickness behaviour. Likewise, if a mouse is injected with BCG, the vaccine against tuberculosis, it passes through a short-term phase of sickness behaviour in the first few days after vaccination but then remains socially isolated from other mice and takes less pleasure in life for many weeks. It looks very much as if the mouse has become chronically depressed as a result of being inflamed.[57]

I say "as if" because I want to stay on guard against the charge of anthropomorphism. We obviously can't know for certain that the mouse feels depressed, or that it can conceive of its own life as more or less pleasurable than it used to be, or that it can imagine that the lives of other mice are more or less pleasurable than its own. All we know is that, under normal circumstances, given a choice between plain water and water that has been sweetened with sugar, mice, like many children, will prefer to drink the sugary liquid. We assume their behavioural preference is motivated by a rewarding sense of pleasure, as we know it is in children. We also know that when the mice are tested again after BCG vaccination, they will no longer prefer to drink sugary water. They have become behaviourally indifferent to the choice before them, and we assume that is because they have lost the hedonistic, pleasure-seeking drive to consume sugar. From their changed behaviour we can infer a change in their mental experience of pleasure, akin to the loss of pleasure or anhedonia that is a core symptom of MDD. Personally, I think this is a reasonably solid line of reasoning that minimises the translational gap between animal and human, and so is not ridiculously anthropomorphic. I can fondly imagine that Descartes himself might have agreed with me, but I can't be sure.

It is philosophically less complicated to focus on animal experiments that tell us something about how inflammation affects the brain, indisputably part of the body machine, than on the behaviour or the inferred mind of the animal. We know that if a dose of bacterial toxin, like LPS, is injected into the bloodstream of a rat, the LPS molecules themselves will not immediately get into the brain. The BBB will keep them out. But the rat's inflammatory response to LPS will penetrate the BBB. Cytokines released from activated macrophages in the rat's body can transmit an inflammatory signal across the BBB that will then activate the macrophages resident in the rat's brain.

For historical reasons, the brain's macrophages are called microglial cells, but despite their different name, microglial cells are very similar to macrophages anywhere else in the body. They spend most of their life waiting quietly for trouble, for a local invasion of hostile agents, or for a broadcast call to arms issued by immune cells under attack in other parts of the body. When microglial cells pick up the inflammatory signals generated by the body in response to an LPS injection, they get angrier, more mobile, and they start pumping out cytokines themselves, effectively echoing or amplifying the body's state of inflammation in the brain. And, as elsewhere in the body, the mobilisation of the brain's microglial robo-cops causes collateral damage to innocent bystanders, to the nerve cells in the surrounding tissue.[58]

When the macrophage army is mobilised under shoot-to-kill orders, whether it is in the lung or the joints or the brain, it will always lay waste to the neighbourhood. The brain is at least spared the scarring that can follow chronic inflammation in other parts of the body – the brain doesn't form mechanically distorting scar tissue in the same way that Mrs P's hands were deformed by fibrous contractures around the joints of her fingers. But the brain suffers from the collateral damage of microglial activation in other ways: nerve cells are more likely to die or to shrink in size, synaptic connections between cells are more likely to be rigid than plastic, and the synaptic supply of neurotransmitters like serotonin is likely to be disrupted.

Not only can angry microglial cells kill nerve cells in their immediate neighbourhood, they can also block the regenerative process that would form new nerve cells in their place. Less extremely, but still seriously, microglial activation can make nerve cells less adaptive, or less plastic. Nerve cells, especially the synaptic connections between nerve cells, are normally plastic. That doesn't mean, for avoidance of doubt, that nerve cells are made of polystyrene or PVC; it means they are malleable or can be remodelled, as if they were made of plasticine. Synaptic connections can be strengthened or weakened, over the course of time, so that the most useful or frequently used connections between nerve cells become stronger and the less useful or usual connections become weaker. Freud was one of the first people to imagine this idea, although he couldn't actually see a synapse or be certain that they existed at the time (Figs. 5 and 8). Now synaptic plasticity is known to be fundamentally important for adaptive behaviour, learning and memory. So the loss of synapses and synaptic plasticity caused by microglial activation provides a plausible explanatory link between inflammation and the memory loss, cognitive impairment and quasi-depressive behaviours observed in inflamed animals.[59]

Microglial activation also has disadvantageous effects on how nerve cells handle the transmitters that pass signals from one cell to another across the synaptic gap. This is especially clear for serotonin, the neurotransmitter that is targeted by SSRIs. Normally nerve cells make serotonin from a raw material called tryptophan. But the cytokines released by angry microglial cells can instruct nerve cells to use this same material to make other end-products, such as kynurenine.[60] This is bad news in two ways. First, it means that there is less serotonin available for release into synapses, so the normal rhythms of serotonin signalling that are thought to be important in controlling sleep, appetite and mood will be disrupted. Second, kynurenine and many of the other molecules produced instead of serotonin are toxic. They poison nerve cells, making them over-excited and metabolically exhausted, and ultimately killing them.

The net effect of microglial activation is that serotonin signalling is disabled and usurped. Bearing in mind the theoretical importance of serotonin for depression, and for how many anti-depressant drugs are supposed to work, these effects of inflammation in animal brains could explain how, at the most fine-grained level of molecules, inflammation can cause depression. When inflammation reduces the amount of serotonin released into synapses, it is effectively pulling in the opposite direction to SSRIs, which are supposed to increase synaptic serotonin levels. This might be one reason why many patients with so-called treatment-resistant depression, who don't respond well to treatment with SSRIs or other anti-depressants, are particularly likely to be inflamed.[61]

MDD in psychiatric patients, and milder depressive symptoms in the general population, are both robustly associated with increased levels of inflammatory proteins in the blood. That much seems beyond doubt from the growing volume of case-control and epidemiological studies that have been published in the last 20 years. Although a psychiatric diagnosis of MDD is conventionally incompatible with bodily disease, the association between MDD and inflammation is mechanistically compatible with the enormous number of medical patients, hiding in plain sight like Mrs P, whose depression arises in the context of an inflammatory disorder of the body.

We also now have strong evidence that inflammation can precede or anticipate depression, which is a necessary condition for inflammation to be causal. And we have increasingly good answers to the how question. We can see how a cytokine signal could get across the barrier between the body and the brain, traditionally regarded as impenetrable. In humans, we can see how even a minor inflammatory shock, like vaccination, can increase activation in regional hotspots of an emotional brain network. In animals, we can see in more detail how inflammation of the body can spread to the brain, activating the brain's own macrophages or microglial cells, and causing collateral damage to nerve cells, synapses, and serotonin metabolism. In humans and mice, at the coarse scale of fMRI and the fine scale of cells and molecules, we can see how inflammation can cause changes in the brain that in turn cause depressive changes in our states of mind or in an animal's behaviour.

This is the tip of an iceberg in the scientific literature and there is much more detail available for those who are interested in knowing more.[4, 10, 12, 62] Yet the hardest Cartesians, the most die-hard dualists, will still not be convinced. They will complain that the evidence is not yet so extraordinarily good as to justify the extraordinary claim that the mind and the body are linked by the immune system. Indeed, to be fair, the mechanistic narrative is not yet crystal clear. There are many loose ends and lacunae, many gaps between what we know about animals and what we know about humans, many results that are based on a few small studies or experimental methods that have quickly become old-fashioned as the science of neuro-immunology has moved forward so fast. But this is the normal state of any rapidly progressing science. And such dramatic recent progress has already brought us to the point where the how question, if not yet entirely solved, looks like an increasingly soluble and sensible question to be asking.

Chapter 6

WHY?

We could know everything there is to know about how inflammation causes depression, and I confidently expect that we will know much more in the next few years; but we would still be left with a sense of incompleteness. There would still be something missing if all we knew was how.

We would still need to know why. Why are some depressed patients inflamed in the first place? And, more generally, why is it that the inflammatory response of the immune system, which is supposed to help us survive in a hostile world, seems to be acting against us, by making us depressed when we are inflamed?

What could make you inflamed (and depressed)?

There are several possible sources of inflammation in the body that could be relevant to depression.

One apparently obvious candidate is inflammatory disease. We now know that depression is common in patients, like Mrs P, who have a major inflammatory or auto-immune disorder such as rheumatoid arthritis, diabetes or atherosclerosis, to name but a few. However, physical disease is an unlikely explanation of the increased levels of cytokines or C-reactive protein (CRP) that have been reported in research studies of major depressive disorder (MDD). This is because, according to the official diagnostic criteria of the American Psychiatric Association, depressed patients can only have a diagnosis of MDD if they do *not* also have a bodily disease. Somewhat bizarrely, in my view, this means that someone like Mrs P, who ticked almost all the diagnostic boxes for depression, cannot, strictly speaking, be said to have an MDD. In clinical practice, the many people in Mrs P's position are most likely to have their mental health symptoms either ignored or diagnosed as a case of so-called "co-morbid" depression. This label of co-morbidity means that their doctors recognise that their depression is associated with an inflammatory disorder like arthritis; and it is therefore not an MDD as psychiatrists have defined it; but neither is it caused by the same pathological process in the immune system that causes the arthritis.

Molière might have recognised co-morbidity as an example of the medical tendency to dress up the patient's symptoms in fancy language without actually explaining where they come from. To this day, a good Cartesian doctor can use the phrase co-morbid depression as a coded way of saying to his patients "Well, you would be, wouldn't you?" *Au contraire*, as we have seen, there is now evidence to suggest that a large proportion of what we're currently calling co-morbid depression, supposedly caused by a purely mental meditation on the sad fact of being diseased, is in fact inflamed depression, mechanistically caused by the very high levels of cytokines and macrophage activity generated by major inflammatory disease.

In any case, by definition, bodily disease cannot explain

where inflammation comes from in patients with MDD. What are some other plausible culprits? Or, to put it more precisely, are there any known risk factors for a psychiatric diagnosis of depression that can also drive increased inflammation?

Body fat, or adipose tissue, is inflammatory. About 60% of the cells in adipose tissue are macrophages, the robocops of the immune system, and one of the principal sources of inflammatory cytokines. Overweight or obese people, with a higher body mass index, will generally have higher blood levels of cytokines and CRP than slimmer people.[62] We also know that overweight people are more likely to be depressed.[63] But is this because obesity causes depression or because depression causes obesity? The causal arrow could point either way, or both ways. Depression could cause behavioural changes, like comfort eating of high-calorie foods, which lead to obesity. Or it could be the other way round. Obesity could cause depression psychologically by exposing people to stressful criticism, and self-criticism, about their physical appearance in our body-shaming culture. Or obesity could cause depression immunologically by increasing the total number of macrophages in the body and increasing the levels of cytokines in the blood. However, it is at least clear that obesity both causes inflammation and increases the risk of depression.

Age, like obesity, is both a cause of increased inflammation and a risk factor for depression. As we grow older, our bodies tend to get more inflamed. Cytokine and CRP levels increase, all other things being equal, over time. Our innate immune system is kept at a steadily increasing level of threat awareness as we grow older.[64] And, as we grow older, we also tend to get more anxious and depressed. Compared to obesity, the causal relationships are a bit clearer. I think we'd all agree that ageing, or at least the passage of time, is not caused by either depression or inflammation. The clock ticks at the same rate whether you're melancholic or not, inflamed or not. So it seems safe to say that increasing age causes increased inflammation, and increased risk of depression, not vice versa. But does this increased inflammation account for all the age-related increase in risk of depression; or is it depressing enough to be aware of your ongoing march to the grave, regardless of your blood cytokine levels? It's not yet safe to say.

Besides age and obesity there are several other possible factors that can both increase inflammation and increase risk of depression. The body's inflammatory status, for example, shows a marked seasonal variation, with higher blood levels of cytokines in European people enduring their winter months of November, December and January, but lower levels during the same months in Australian people enjoying a southern-hemisphere summer.[65] Evidently the immune system is more prone to become inflamed in winter, presumably because the risk of flu or other infectious diseases is increased in winter, which is also a time of increased risk of depressive symptoms, especially for people with seasonal affective disorder. Is that a coincidence, or could seasonal or circadian rhythms in the immune system be driving annual or daily mood swings? We don't know, yet.

As you can see, neuro-immunology is still too young a science to have answered all the questions it has begun to ask. But, intriguingly, one of the clearest leads to have emerged so far as a plausible source of bodily inflammation in depressed people is not a physical factor, like age or obesity or hours of daylight. It is a social factor.

Flaming stressed

Stress is both one of the most well-known, and one of the least well-understood, causes of depression. It is a familiar fact of life, which all of us probably have experienced at first or second hand, that stressful events can make people depressed. The epidemiological research confirms that this is a massive effect, especially for some kinds of stress, so-called major life events, like death of a spouse or parent or child, or loss of a job, or some other bereavement or humiliation. Your chances of becoming depressed under those circumstances are up to nine-fold greater than the background risk of depression.[66] To turn it around the other way, about 80% of all episodes of depression have been preceded by a stressful life event.[67] The most depressing stresses are events that involve both loss of an important relationship and social rejection. So a man who has initiated divorce proceedings against his wife will be at 10 times greater risk of depression, because of the loss of the marital relationship; but a man who is being divorced by his wife will be at 20 times greater risk of depression, because the loss of his marriage is compounded by the humiliation of being dumped.[68]

The impact of stress on risk for depression couldn't be clearer. What has not been so clear is *how* social stress can have such a catastrophic effect on depression. There is, as always, the good Cartesian view that you would be, wouldn't you? If your wife had gone off with somebody else, if you'd just been fired, I bet you wouldn't be too happy either. But, as always, that isn't scientifically illuminating, or therapeutically helpful. It can imply that becoming depressed in response to stress is a personal choice, or evidence of an insufficiently stoic character, or in some other way one's own fault. The pain of the stress is compounded by the shame of a moral failure to get over it. The last 20 years have witnessed a remarkable growth in support for an alternative explanation, based on the body's inflammatory response, rather than the mind's introspective reflections.

One of the first clues that major life events can have an impact on the immune system was the actuarial fact that life expectancy is reduced by bereavement.[69] If your wife divorces you, or you suffer some other horrible event in your life, not only will you be at very high risk of depression, you will also be more likely to develop cancer or heart disease, and your predicted lifespan will be shorter than it was before the event. We talk about dying of a broken heart as if it was merely a figure of speech but we know it is happening all around us: people are dying younger than we'd expect following the loss of a loved one. I have heard many stories of a long-married couple dying within a few weeks of each other. Haven't we all? And a recent study confirmed that the risk of death due to a heart attack or stroke is doubled in someone who has recently been bereaved.[70] The emotional and social shock of losing your life-long partner has a massively negative effect on your fitness to survive. Insurance companies know this well. It is why they offer bereavement counselling to their customers. Grief can kill you. It's another stubborn fact that could have an immunological explanation.

We now know that a stressful life event throws a rock in the pond of the immune system, causing major changes in how all the different types of immune cell are working and interacting with each other.[71, 72] The macrophages of the innate immune system, patrolling the front line of the self, are made angry or more activated by bereavement, and pump more inflammatory cytokines into the circulation.[73] The excessive activity of the macrophages could inflame athero-sclerotic arteries, increasing the risk of blood clots forming in the blood vessels of the heart or the brain, and thus making a heart attack or stroke more likely. The impact of social stress on the immune system is one explanation for how you could die of a broken heart.

Social stresses less singular and extreme than a bereavement can also cause inflammatory activation of macrophages.[14] Biomarkers of inflammation, like cytokines and CRP, are increased in many stressful situations, including poverty, debt and social isolation. Carers of patients with Alzheimer's disease, people with day-to-day responsibility for a spouse or relative with dementia, have increased inflammatory biomarkers.[74] So do adults who suffered poverty, neglect or maltreatment as children.

An important epidemiological study from New Zealand followed a cohort of 1,037 children born in 1972–73 in the city of Dunedin.[15] The children were carefully assessed for their socio-economic status (roughly speaking, the wealth of their parents), their social isolation and their experience of maltreatment. When they were reassessed as adults 30 years later, it was found that the incidence of inflammation, depression and obesity was approximately twice as high in the adults who had been impoverished, isolated or abused as children. We have known for decades that the immune system has a long-term memory for childhood infections or vaccinations. Now we are beginning to understand that the immune system could also be able to remember childhood episodes of assault or famine or any other severe threat to the self's early survival. Child abuse survivors may enter adult life with their immune system set on a hair-trigger, poised to react to minor infections and social setbacks with a disproportionate inflammatory response that causes depressive symptoms. There could perhaps be a novel, immune-related explanation for the adverse effects of childhood abuse on adult mental health, effects that were first courageously recognised by Freud (and Breuer) more than 100 years ago.

But you don't have to be depressed, bereaved or abused to know what social stress is like. There are some things that almost everyone finds stressful to some degree, and public speaking is one of them. Standing up in front of a lot of people to talk to them all at once, even for a few minutes, almost always causes a subjective sense of apprehension or anxiety, accompanied by an objective bodily state of arousal with increased blood pressure, heart rate and sweating. The body's response to public speaking is a muted form of its fight-or-flight response to many different challenges: to pump up adrenaline and noradrenaline, to activate the sympathetic nervous system. And, at the same time, to ramp down the calming, anti-adrenaline effects of the vagus nerve. For some people, this adrenalised, anxious state is so aversive they just won't put themselves through it. Being asked questions in public, as we medical students were interrogated on the wards at Bart's, is also stressful. Even people who now seem to be very comfortable with public speaking, very quick on their feet with questions, will often have worked hard in the past to master their automatic, reflexive anxieties about doing it. That much we have known about the stress of public speaking for a long time. What has only become known more recently is that even relatively minor stresses like public speaking cause rapid inflammatory activation of the body.

The Trier social stress test is designed to simulate the challenge of public speaking in an experimentally controlled way. The experimental subject or participant is asked to address an audience of four people for 12 minutes and is then tested by members of the audience on mental arithmetic questions for four minutes. Often the experiment is set up so that the participant speaks from a standing position in front of a table, on the other side of which is seated the audience, each of them wearing a white lab coat and a dissatisfied expression. We can probably all imagine how stressful this experience will be for the participants – even though they know consciously that it is not for real, it is an ethically approved experiment, and nothing can go seriously wrong for them as a result of their performance.

A group of happy and healthy schoolteachers, who felt professionally satisfied by their work in German schools in the 1990s, participated in a recent study which required them to provide two blood samples for testing, once before and once after they had done the Trier social stress test.[75] The macrophages circulating in their blood were significantly more activated, were pumping out more cytokines, immediately after public speaking than they had been before. And then the experiment was repeated with a second group of school-teachers, who were professionally frustrated by their work. Teaching is a notoriously stressful job, with high levels of early retirement and absence due to sickness, and this second group of teachers felt that the effort they were putting into their work was not adequately rewarded; the burden of their responsibilities was not compensated by money, promotion, or the respect of their students and colleagues. They were still managing to come in to work but they were burning out. The macrophages of the burnt-out teachers were angrier than the macrophages of the happy teachers before the test; and they became even angrier as a result of the added stress of public speaking.

We don't yet know for sure exactly how a stressful event, like public speaking, could activate the immune system but there are a couple of plausible ideas under investigation. For example, we know that the adrenaline rush in response to stress sends a danger signal to macrophages, triggering the same kind of angry response as a signal of dangerous infection like LPS. We also know that stress can interfere with the hormonal system in the body, making macrophages less responsive to the calming effects of steroids.[10] There are many details still to resolve, as always, but that's one of the fascinating things about science: every step forward generates more questions.

Causal chains and circles

Stringing it all together, we can now claim to understand how inflammation causes depression, and where that inflammation could come from in the first place. We can construct a simple linear narrative, tell a story with a beginning, a middle and an end. Once upon a time, there was stress, which caused inflammation, and then depression, in the end. That could be how stress causes depression. That's now a plausible and testable mechanistic hypothesis that deserves further investigation, especially in relation to the development of new treatments for depression.

But it could also be possible for the causal relationships between stress, inflammation and depression to be circular rather than linear.[76] It is not unusual for patients to find that their depression puts them under greater social stress – being depressed they are more likely to be socially withdrawn and lacking energy. They will almost certainly suffer some degree of stigmatisation, their most supportive relationships may deteriorate, they may lose income or economic status, they may become more reliant on state benefits. In other words, there are many social ways in which depression can cause stress, to add to the neuro-immunological ways we now know by which stress can cause depression.

It could be a vicious cycle. Greater exposure to early severe stress – like child abuse – could increase the body's natural tendency to become inflamed in response to social stresses later in life. Increased inflammation in response to stress could drive greater changes in the brain, causing more severe depression. Then the depression itself – the diagnosis and treatment of MDD – could act to increase the risk of more stress arising in the future, and so on, and on.

I can recall seeing a patient, a young woman, who had been sexually abused by her stepfather between the ages of 11 and 13. She had some minor depressive symptoms in adolescence, as many young women do, but she seemed to be OK. Then he died, when she was in her twenties, which brought it all back to the surface, and out into the open with her family, and triggered a major depressive disorder. For a while she was very unwell – she hated and seriously harmed herself, believing that her stepfather was Satan and she must follow him into hell. She was admitted to a psychiatric hospital for treatment against her will. When she came out, four months later, she was better, at first, less depressed when I asked her the usual questions in the outpatient clinic. But she'd lost her place in the world. She'd lost the flat she was renting with friends. She'd missed deadlines for job applications. Her family was still torn apart by the impact of her stepfather's death. Many professionals and other people tried to help. But she was adrift, socially stressed by her isolation, and it wasn't long before she was back in hospital, this time with greater suicidal determination. She tried all the usual anti-depressant drugs, without much obvious benefit. In the end, I am sure it was her family coming back together, and supporting her, that did the most to help her recovery.

Now when I think back on her story – which is not an unusual kind of story in mental health services – I wonder how much of it could have an inflammatory angle. Were her blood and brain macrophages activated by the abuse, primed to kick off throughout her adolescence, and then explosively reactivated by the stress of her abuser's death? Is that why she became depressed the first time? And were her macrophages still on high alert, like those of burnt-out schoolteachers, when she encountered new social stresses, coming out of hospital? Like schoolteachers doing the Trier social stress test, did she have an inflammatory over-reaction to the additional stress, of social demotion and disorientation, caused by her first depression? Is that why she became depressed the second time? In her case, we'll never know for sure if such a positive feedback loop was cycling viciously from stress to inflammation to depression and back to stress. It didn't cross our minds at the time. We never thought about inflammation, or did blood tests for immune biomarkers, in psychiatric outpatient clinics back then.

In future, I think we will know more about the circular logic of stress, inflammation and depression, and we should be able to use this knowledge to make a difference to treatment of depression (Fig. 12). But this still won't address the ultimate question: why does inflammation cause depression?

Ultimately, the answer must always be Darwin

When it comes to biological systems – or life as we know it, scientifically – the answer to the question "why?" is always the same: natural selection. Why do finches have differently shaped beaks on the different islands of the Galapagos archipelago? Why do some orchids produce flowers that look like bees? Why does an elephant have tusks or a tiger have stripes? The ultimate reason for any biological phenomenon or phenotype to appear in life, or to disappear into the fossil record, is that it is more or less adaptive, more or less likely to make an organism fit to survive. Random genetic mutations constantly generate minor variations on the theme of existing species. If some genetic mutations happen, by chance, to make the organism more adaptive, more resilient, or in any other way more reproductively successful, then the mutated form of the gene will be naturally selected for onward transmission to future generations, and the species will slowly evolve along the trajectory coded by expression of the selected gene. The standard answer to the why question for tiger stripes is that the first tiger with a mutant pigment gene that randomly produced camouflage stripes turned out to be less vulnerable to predators or rival tigers, more likely to survive and reproduce, so that the stripy mutation was naturally selected in generation after generation as the species evolved to the point that all tigers were striped.

That is the modern evolutionary synthesis, the biggest idea in biology, the bringing-together of genetics and the Darwinian principle of natural selection, which can explain why almost everything in life is as it is. Can it help us answer the general question: why are so many of us depressed? Or the more mechanistic question: why does the immune system cause people to become depressed?

If you ask Google about Darwin and depression, the top-ranked hits will not lead you to his evolutionary theory of depression but to other people's theories about *his* depression. Charles Darwin suffered all sorts of symptoms throughout his adult life, both bodily symptoms like vomiting and flatulence, and mental symptoms like panic and fatigue. He couldn't cope with the stress of public speaking in defence of his controversial ideas and he never had what you might call a proper job. He secluded himself from the world, living quietly on his private income in an old rectory outside London, writing his books about earthworms, barnacles and the origin of species. While he was alive, he baffled the many physicians he consulted but found some relief from spa treatments, homeopathy and a diet without dairy products.

Even after his death, the origin of Darwin's illness has remained a surprisingly lively topic. At least 30 different diagnoses have been proposed, ranging from postural hypotension to lactose intolerance and melancholia. One of the more exotic ideas is that he picked up a nasty infection, called Chagas disease, when he was bitten by the "great black bug of the Pampas" while exploring Argentina on his voyage on HMS *Beagle*. It's a story that might seem to suit my story well: one can imagine a chronic bacterial infection like Chagas disease causing inflammation which in turn caused Darwin's social withdrawal and other depressive behaviours when he returned to England. But one moral of my story is that we need biomarkers to make a diagnosis of inflamed depression. Despite some recent, misguided attempts to exhume Darwin's body from his grave in Westminster Abbey for DNA testing, we don't have any biomarkers on him. And personally I think we should let his bones rest in peace.

There is less confusion about Darwin's interest in insanity than there is about his own state of mind. As a young man, he discussed cases of madness with his father, a physician, and in later life he corresponded extensively with Henry Maudsley, the 19th-century English psychiatrist who founded the hospital named after him in London. What Darwin wanted to know from Maudsley, and the other asylum superintendents he corresponded with, was what their patients looked like, what facial expressions were characteristic of melancholia or mania.

Darwin held the view that human emotions were expressed by, or might even be caused by, contraction of facial muscles, and that these muscular mechanisms for emotional expression were inherited by descent from animals. This is an idea that might seem easy to endorse these days. Yes, of course, we can tell if people are happy or sad by whether they're smiling or frowning. And many people believe that they can tell by a dog's or a horse's facial expression if it is feeling bored or anxious or surprised. Darwin's idea of "grief muscles", which cause emotion by expressing it in the face, is even compatible with the recent discovery that Botox injections, used cosmetically to iron out the wrinkles of ageing by paralysing facial muscles, have strong anti-depressant effects.[77]

However, this idea of emotional expression has some troubling implications from a Cartesian perspective. If human emotions are expressed or generated by bodily mechanisms, inherited by descent from lower animals, then they cannot be the province of the mind or soul. Darwin's ideas about the facial expression of emotions pushed his evolutionary theory close to the heart of human nature and provided a material explanation for fine feelings that many of his contemporaries would have preferred to believe had a spiritual meaning. Darwin managed the prospect of ideological conflict, which he did not enjoy, by amassing copious quantities of data. Reasoning that "the insane ought to be studied as they are liable to the strongest passions and give vent to them", he included second-hand descriptions, and pioneered the use of photographs, provided by Maudsley and others, to convey the facial expressions of the inmates of their asylums in his book *The Expression of the Emotions in Man and Animals*.[78] (Fig 11).

Darwin used clinical data on "the insane" to inform his thinking about evolution. But what he did not do was turn things around and try using evolutionary theory to inform our thinking about the origins of insanity. Darwin and Maudsley were both well aware that psychiatric disorders tended to run in families and were therefore heritable. Darwin was worried about the risk of insanity arising in his own large family because of his consanguineous marriage to his cousin Emma. Maudsley, like Kraepelin and other psychiatrists of the time, could see patterns of familial clustering and generational transmission in large asylum populations of schizophrenia, manic-depressive insanity, psychopathy and a myriad other diagnostically labelled cases.

According to Darwinian theory, a melancholic or depressive disposition, like any other trait that passed from one generation to another, must be subject to natural selection and must somehow make depressed people fitter and more likely to survive. But that is counter-intuitive and counterfactual: we know that serious mental [sic] illness is a mortal blow to fitness, as witnessed by the 15-year cut to life expectancy of patients with schizophrenia and bipolar disorder in the UK in 2018. On the face of it, there is no survival advantage, no competitive edge, no reproductive reward for serious mental illness. So how has it come to be? How has depression evolved, if not to make us fitter?

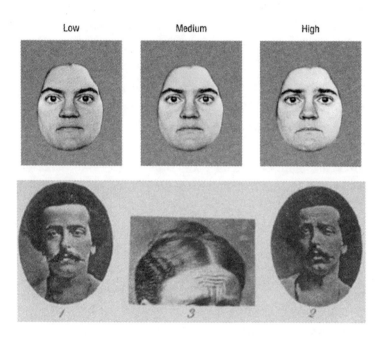

Low   Medium   High

Figure 11: Emotional faces and emotional brains. Darwin collected observations on patients with melancholia and other species of insanity from the well-stocked asylums of eminent European neurologists and psychiatrists. He paid particular attention to the orientation of the eyebrows, and the pattern of muscular ridges and furrows between them, the omega sign, so called because it was supposed to look like Ω. More than 100 years later, the standard test faces chosen to express a normal range of sadness for fMRI research studies are still Darwinian in their focus on eyebrow angle as a signal of mood. As Darwin might have predicted, but never knew, the saddest faces cause the strongest activation of an emotional brain network that we have inherited by descent from other animals.

The heritability of mental disorders posed a question for natural selection that Darwin didn't get to before he died. Maudsley, on the other hand, had time to answer the question more explicitly, but in a non-Darwinian way that took us in totally the wrong direction for about 50 disastrous years. He was one of many *fin de siècle* psychiatrists who thought that the progression of mental disorders and criminal types from one generation to another was not dictated by Darwinian natural selection but by an earlier theory of evolution, proposed by Jean-Baptiste Lamarck, who died a few years before the young Darwin set out on his voyage on HMS *Beagle* in 1831. Lamarck can be credited with writing the first biological theory of evolution, the first step away from the Old Testament's assertion that all the plant and animal species of life were divinely created and therefore eternally unchanging. Lamarck's theory expected life forms to change, to become increasingly complex, to evolve; but to do so by the inheritance of acquired characteristics, rather than by the selection of randomly mutated genes.

Let's say that, before you were born, your father had acquired the characteristic of drinking heavily: that bad habit of his could have a detrimental effect on your genetic inheritance. According to Lamarckism, you would inherit a higher risk of becoming an alcoholic because your father had got into the habit of drinking heavily. And your alcoholism would have a similar but greater detrimental effect on the moral character and psychiatric risks of your children. A crude but common rule of thumb in 19th-century psychiatry was that alcoholism in the first generation would lead to madness in the second and idiocy in the third. The Lamarckian mechanism was supposed to drive an escalating degenerative process, so that each generation's psychiatric, criminal and moral misbehaviours were recapitulated and magnified in the next.

You could say that it was their neglect of natural selection as a possible answer to the question – why is there mental illness? – that led Maudsley, Kraepelin and many others to make ethically unacceptable recommendations for social cleansing of psychiatrically degenerate lines or races. It was not only in Germany that eugenic thinking was strong in psychiatry and medicine between about 1880 and 1940, a period of time that is now called Darwin's eclipse, when natural selection was largely forgotten and ideas of social selection prevailed brutally. We all know how those ideas played out politically and psychiatrically. There is no reason to go that way again.

The end of Darwin's eclipse roughly coincided with the emergence of the modern evolutionary synthesis, in the 1940s and 50s. This is the big idea, now as close to axiomatic as it gets in biology or medicine, that evolution is entirely explained by natural selection of genes. Thinking afresh about the heritability of depression, in this neo-Darwinian context, we come back to the same question: what is the survival advantage of depression? The answer is still the same: there is none.

People with major depression, on average, live shorter lives, are more likely to have chronic medical disorders, are more likely to be unemployed, or less likely to be highly productive if they do have a job. Crucially, depressed people are likely to have fewer children, and the children of depressed parents are slower to achieve normal growth milestones. Not only is there no social or material advantage to major depression in this life, there is no obvious advantage to the next generation, and ultimately no promise of immortality for the genes involved in making these depressive behaviours unfold over untold generations. You might think, on the face of it, genes for depression should have been selected out of the population millennia ago; we should by now have reached the sunlit uplands where the shadow of melancholia never falls. But we haven't. And I doubt we ever will. So there must be something good about being depressed; there must be some advantage to depression that accounts for its natural selection, but what is it?

A savannah survival story

We can make this question a lot easier to answer if we change the wording slightly. Instead of asking what is the survival advantage of depression, let's ask ourselves what *was* the survival advantage of depression? Maybe the genes that code for depressive behaviours were naturally selected millions of years ago because being depressed then was somehow advantageous in a way that it isn't now? We know that many human brain genes are ancient, like the gene for the serotonin receptor that goes back as far as the humble nematode worms, like *C elegans*, which evolved at least 500 million years ago. So it makes sense that there should be a lag time in evolution. Once a gene has been selected in a worm, or a dog, or an ancestral caveman, let's say, it will often stick around, or be conserved, in the modern human genome. So we may find ourselves doing genetically programmed things in 2018 that made perfect sense on the ancestral savannah but don't seem to be working out so well here and now.

OK, we don't know much about the ancestral savannah, still less about the selection pressures on pre-human apes and mammals. We weren't there at the time. And we can't very easily do experiments on evolutionary processes that have been ongoing for hundreds of millions of years. We have to make up stories about what might have happened. Then try to test our best guess scientifically. As it happens, some of the most compelling (and testable) recent evolutionary theories of depression have focused on natural selection of genes controlling the immune system.[9, 10]

The story is generally told about tribes of early humans struggling to survive on the African plains about 150,000 years ago. It would have been a harsh challenge indeed to find enough food, to survive attacks by predators and rival tribes, to find a mate, to raise a family. There were many threats to survival but number one was infection. Life provided many opportunities for infection, like childbirth, injuries and wounds, and there was very little effective treatment. The infant mortality rate was high, the maternal death rate in pregnancy and childbirth was high, and the men involved in hunting and fighting usually died in their twenties. A lot of this attrition was due to infectious diseases that started trivially with a cut hand, or at the stump of a roughly severed umbilical cord. And there were also contagious infections, plagues, that passed from person to person, and could decimate a tribe. Obviously, anything that the body can do in terms of defence against infection is highly advantageous in this context. You can imagine that gene mutations that made the macrophages slightly angrier, or that made cytokine signalling slightly stronger, could be advantageous if they strengthened the front-line defences of the innate immune system against the bacterial killers that attack babies and young children. Genes that have randomly mutated to deliver enhanced killing power against germs will be naturally selected because people who have inherited them will be more likely to survive childhood and reach the repro-ductively active stage of life at puberty. In an environment like the ancestral savannah, with a high infant mortality rate due to infection, there will be a strong natural-selection pres-sure on genes that boost innate inflammatory response.

Those inflammatory genes could help people survive in many ways. They could increase rates of wound healing and reduce the risk of a local infection becoming global. They could also change behaviour. In much the same way as an infected animal, a wounded or sick human, like me after root canal work, shows a characteristic pattern of behaviour. Ill or invalid human beings withdraw from social contact, reduce their physical activity, eat less, and are less hedonic. They are also quietly anxious and have disturbed sleep. This is a very engrained and consistent pattern of behaviour, written into our DNA by genes that must have evolved millions of years before *H sapiens*. As we have seen, this sickness behaviour is strongly driven by innate inflammatory mechanisms. So the genes that are naturally selected to defeat infection by killing bugs on the front line can also be expected to drive sickness behaviour. But how could sickness behaviour be an advantage for survival on the savannah?

We can imagine that temporary withdrawal from the tribe could protect our ill ancestor, the "patient", from demanding social obligations and competition at a time when he needs to rest and use all his resources to fight off infection. In this comforting vision, the isolated patient is protected, licensed to do very little but recover. Loss of appetite could also favour survival by preventing him from wasting energy on digestion or searching for food at a time when all the biological energy in his body must be commandeered to activate the macrophage army in the all-consuming fight against infection. This makes sickness behaviour sound like genetically programmed convalescence: a good thing for the patient, designed to hasten his recovery. But we can also imagine that sickness behaviour had another, less comfortable side to it, out there on the savannah. When night fell, and the rest of the tribe was gathered around a fire and food, the isolated patient could easily be forgotten in the marginal shadows where predators lurked. If the tribe was attacked by a rival tribe, or forced to migrate because of drought, the patient would likely be among the first casualties, exposed at the edge of the group. Isolation would increase the external threats to him. So sickness behaviours of anxiety and sleep disturbance might be advantageous to his survival by keeping him alert to danger, even while all he wanted to do was rest and heal his septic wound.

The key sickness behaviour of social withdrawal is thus both protective and threatening for the patient. But for the tribe it is more purely protective. Contagious disease was a special threat to ancestral tribes, which were originally not much more than extended families of a few hundred, highly interrelated people. Disease could spread rapidly and the genetic similarity between tribal members would mean that if a germ proved lethal to one of them it would likely be lethal to them all. A catastrophic plague could wipe out the entire tribal gene pool. By isolating the patient, the innate immune behaviour of social withdrawal reduces the risk that currently uninfected but genetically related members of the tribe will also become infected. You can think about social withdrawal as a form of quarantine. The patient's inflamed behaviour puts him at anxiety-provoking risk of being picked off at the margins, for the sake of making the tribe as a whole more resilient to contagious infection. You can imagine that sickness behaviour was naturally selected as much for the survival of the tribal DNA as for the patient's individual DNA. You could say that natural selection has picked genes that will drive an infected individual to put himself at risk for the common good. The 15th-century leper colony visited by Paracelsus on the edge of Nuremberg is a more modern example of the tribe's highly conserved instinct to protect itself from contagion, by quarantining or excluding potentially infectious invalids.

In any case, as the savannah story would have it, at some point in the deep time of human prehistory, genes were selected to increase the inflammatory response to infection, so that our ancestors, or at least our ancestral tribes, were more likely to survive. Selecting more inflammatory genes makes sense in terms of accelerating and magnifying the body's rapid rebuttal of an actual infection. But you can imagine that it would be even more advantageous to select genes that could *predict* an infectious threat, as well as respond to infection aggressively once it had occurred.

If the macrophage army was revved up before the first hostile germs invaded that would give it a much better chance of wiping out the infection before the enemy started multiplying and the infection became more serious. Out on the savannah, we can imagine that infection was strongly predicted by trauma, by injuries or wounds, often sustained in hunting or fighting. Since even a minor combat wound could be complicated by fatal infection, it would make sense to select genes to detect socially competitive or dangerous situations and to alert the immune system to be prepared for an imminent risk of infection. Then the ancestral patient's body would already be inflamed before he was injured by his tribal enemy, and before his macrophages saw their bacterial enemy for the first time.

This is a story about our evolution that could help us answer the question why. We have inherited genes that will accentuate all aspects of innate inflammation, including depressive behaviour, in response to actual or threatened infections. And the same genes that conferred a survival advantage in response to the fact or threat of infection, on the savannah, have passed down to us many generations on as apparently disadvantageous genes that make us more inflamed in response to social conflict, and more depressed in response to inflammation.

Mrs P might have been prone to experience depressive symptoms in response to the surge in cytokines kicked off by her joint disease because she had inherited genes that kept an ancestor alive after childbirth 100,000 years ago. The burnt-out teachers might have been at risk of becoming inflamed in response to the various social threats of life in the metaphorical jungle of a modern classroom because they inherited genes that had protected their ancestors against post-traumatic infection when they were fighting a rival tribe in the real jungle. One might even wonder if the stigmatisation of depression in 2018 is somehow related to the isolation of ancestral tribe members who were behaving as if they were inflamed. Could the common feeling that "we don't know what to say" to our depressed friend conceal an ancient inherited instinct to recoil from close contact with people who are behaving as if they are inflamed and potentially infectious?

The savannah story is seductive because it seems plausible, and it is aligned with neo-Darwinian theory, as it sweeps seamlessly from wounded hunter-gatherers to stressed-depressed patients in the NHS. But it is only one of many plausible evolutionary rationales, or "just so stories" as some scientists sceptically call them, that you could make up to explain the survival value of depression. We need to test the savannah story, somehow, to be sure that it's more than a story.

We can't experimentally rerun human evolution in a germ-free environment, from the birth of *C elegans* 500 million years ago, to show that without ancestral exposure to infection the genes that cause inflamed depression in *H sapiens* in the 21st century would not have been selected. However, that is not to say the story can't be tested scientifically at all. If the savannah survival story is true then at least some of the genes that increase risk for depression should be genes that control the immune system, and that is a prediction we can test experimentally in the real world.

We know that depression is heritable – it runs in families – so your risk of being depressed is increased approximately three-fold if both your parents are depressed and increased approximately two-fold if one or more of your siblings is depressed. However, depression is not as strongly heritable as some other psychiatric disorders, like schizophrenia or bipolar disorder. And that may be part of the reason why the individual genes that underpin the heritability of depression have proven more difficult to identify than the genes for schizophrenia or Alzheimer's disease. It is also likely that depression, like many other common and heritable disorders, is not determined by one or two genes with strongly adverse effects on brain and mind phenotypes, but by many genes, each contributing a small quantum of risk for depression. To find many genes of weak effect in a moderately heritable disorder means we have to test all 20,000 genes in the whole genome, not just a few genes; and that in turn means we need to collect data on very large numbers of patients. It is a numbers game and psychiatric genetics has only very recently amassed big enough numbers on depression.

Some of the first major studies that searched the whole genome for genes that increased the risk of depression drew a blank. They found nothing, no significant differences in the frequency of different DNA variations between patients with depression and healthy volunteers. But although these studies seemed big at the time, comprising data on tens of thousands of patients, it turns out that the reason they failed to find anything was that they were not big enough. Very recently, in a study that has only just been published online, a large international consortium of investigators analysed DNA from about 130,000 cases of depression and 330,000 healthy controls. They found 44 genes that were significantly associated with depression.[79] At last, for the first time, in 2018, we are closing in on the genetic roots of melancholia.

What are these genes and what do they do? Many of them are genes that are known to be important for the nervous system, which is not surprising to those of us who expect mood states to be generated by the brain. More remarkably, many of them are also known to be important for the immune system. For example, the single gene most significantly associated with depression is one called olfactomedin 4. Until it emerged at the top of the risk list for depression, this gene was best known for its role in controlling the gut's inflammatory response to dangerous bacteria.[80] People who have inherited a mutation in olfactomedin 4 that makes their stomach wall more inflamed by bacterial infection might benefit from some survival advantage in terms of resistance to stomach ulceration; but they are also more likely to become depressed. This is a brand-new result, yet to be scrutinised scientifically in detail, but it is robustly based on a huge amount of data, and it is pretty much as predicted by the savannah survival story, which is maybe not so "just so" after all.

——◦▢◦◦▢◦——

Scepticism is the first Cartesian principle of science and it keeps us honest. The history of medicine and psychiatry is littered with discredited treatments that got away with it for a while because of insufficient professional scepticism. But what is left to support a sceptical position about the links between inflammation and depression?

It is now clear beyond reasonable doubt that they are linked, and that they can be causally linked. We can draw an explanatory path from bodily inflammation, across the blood brain barrier, to inflamed brain cells and networks, which ultimately cause the mood and behavioural changes of depression. We know that bodily inflammation can come from social stress, which is a well-known risk for depression. We can imagine that this linkage between stress, inflammation and depression could have been advantageous to our ancestors in their fight against infection. And there is some evidence just emerging that genes controlling the inflammatory response to infection, and presumably first selected for that reason back on the savannah, are also risk genes for depression in the modern world.

Of course, you can, if you wish, suspend judgment on the grounds that the data are not yet compelling, there are still a lot of wrinkles to iron out, what it really needs is another experiment, etc. But the shrink in me would say: are you sure your reasonable reservations are not an unconscious defence of your Cartesian blind spot? As the great man so nearly said, the more progressive philosophy is surely *immuno ergo sum*.

Chapter 7

SO WHAT?

Change can come slowly to medicine. It is a highly regulated and professionally conservative business, and there are overwhelmingly good reasons for that. Nonetheless, it can be frustrating. Countless people have noticed a link between inflammation and depression in their own lives. It is not uncommon to become seriously depressed after breaking a bone, or to experience mood swings that oscillate in sync with the exacerbations and remissions of inflammatory bowel disease. Chronic fatigue syndrome, which has some features in common with depression, can follow glandular fever, a viral infection of lymphocytes in adolescence. The menopausal transition, which is associated with a high rate of depression and anti-depressant drug use among mid-life women, is also associated with an increase in peripheral inflammation.[81] And it is not only biological factors that can affect both mood states and the immune system. Social factors, like adversity or conflict, can also cause inflammation, which might help to explain the very frequent experience of depression being triggered by adult or childhood stress.

But what practical advice can contemporary scientific medicine offer on this theoretical basis? What kind of advanced services might be available for treatment of the inflamed mind? To manage expectations up front, we should think positive in the medium term, but know that the treatment options for inflamed depression are limited at the time of writing (2018).

Many patients struggle to access healthcare that is joined up, between body and mind, across the old Cartesian fault-line. Physicians often prefer looking at X-rays to making eye contact; psychiatrists have been trained to leave their stethoscopes at home. It is very difficult, at least in the British NHS in 2018, for a patient with inflamed depression (or dementia or psychosis) to find a clinical service that will deal in an even-handed way with both the physical and mental aspects of their condition. There is talk, at a high level in governments and other important bodies, about "parity of esteem" between physical health and mental health. People working in NHS mental health services would love to believe that this is more than just an inspiring phrase. But there is not yet much sign of integrated and equitable delivery of specialist physical and mental health services to patients.

Arguably, the medical profession has been slow to acknowledge the importance of such an integrated approach to physical and mental health, not at all because individual doctors or scientists are incompetent or negligent or heartless, but because the well-trained eye has a Cartesian blind spot. Like all blind spots, this both blinds us to something (that's hiding in plain sight) and blinds us to our blindness. We can't see something and we can't see that we can't see it.

Neuro-immunology has begun to give us new insight into how and why the immune system can link body and mind. But so what? What can we do with this new knowledge that could really make a difference to the experiences of people with depression?

The immune perspective on depression could open up several possible new lines of treatment. Development of anti-inflammatory drugs and antibodies, as next generation anti-depressants, is one obvious way to go. It is also likely that immunological thinking will increasingly influence the development of new drug treatments for other brain and mental health disorders, like Alzheimer's disease and schizophrenia. But recognising the causal links between body, brain and mind that are mediated by the immune system does not lead only to new drug treatments, and is not relevant only to biotech and pharmaceutical companies. Neuro-immunology could inform the development and optimisation in practice of other treatments that are more attractive to the many depressed patients who don't like taking drugs and the many mental health practitioners who don't like prescribing them. Bearing in mind what we now know about how the vagus nerve controls inflammation, maybe we could use nerve-stimulating devices to treat inflamed depression? And recalling the crucial importance of stress for both inflammation and depression, maybe we can monitor the effectiveness of psychological and social interventions by inflammatory biofeedback?

I am uncharacteristically bullish about the chances of progress (Fig. 12). But none of this has yet happened; and we can't be sure it ever will happen until it has actually begun to make a real difference to the experience of being clinically depressed.

Medical apartheid

These days, specialist medical services are routinely split down the middle, following the Cartesian divide between body and mind. Patients see a physician, who attends to the physical aspects of their disorder, or they see a psychiatrist or psychologist, who attends to the mental aspects. Physicians and psychiatrists are separately trained as specialists in one or other of the dualist domains. Cross-talk is not encouraged. Physicians are expected to acquire deep expertise in the biological mechanisms of physical health disorders but have a licence to ignore mental health. Psychiatrists are expected to have esoteric knowledge about the psychological causes of mental health disorders but not to be competent in matters of physical health. I am caricaturing, but slightly. I saw both sides of the divide in the space of about six months in 1989 as I transitioned from the end of my training as a physician, when I learnt that it was professionally OK to do nothing about mental health symptoms, in a case like Mrs P, to the start of my training as a psychiatrist, when I learnt that it was professionally suspect to do anything about physical health symptoms.

For the first few months of my new life as a psychiatrist, I brought my stethoscope to work with me, which was immediately regarded as eccentric, and I couldn't help noticing that many of the so-called mental patients on the wards had undiagnosed or untreated physical disorders. I remember seeing a man who had been diagnosed as having panic attacks and alcohol dependence. Reading through his notes, I could see

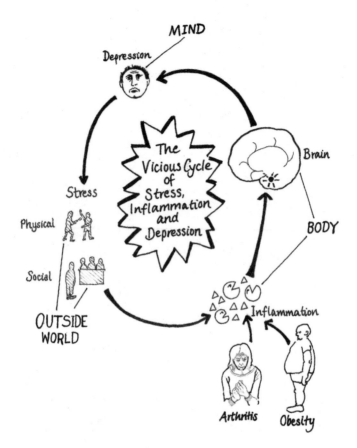

Figure 12: The vicious cycle of stress, inflammation and depression – and ways to break it – an artist's impression. Inflammation can change how the brain works, which causes mood changes and depressive disorders, which increase the risk of social stresses, which cause bodily inflammation, and so on. There could be several ways to break this vicious cycle. In a dualist world, depression is all in the mind and treatment is psychological. Since the 1950s, we have in practice also often treated depression with drugs that act on the brain. Stress relief or control is an expected benefit of meditation or mindfulness training; but major causes of social stress, like poverty

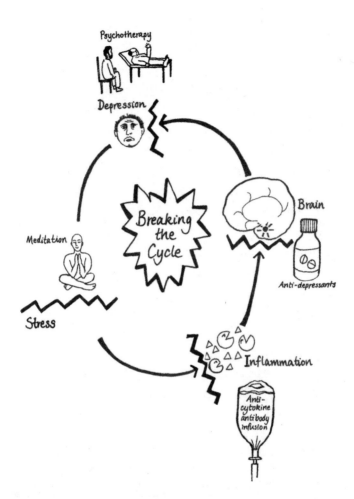

or abuse, are not easily soluble. The new therapeutic idea is that we could also try breaking this vicious cycle, as it passes through the body, by targeting the inflammatory links between depression and social stress as well as between depression and bodily disorders like arthritis and obesity. This could mean re-purposing drugs, like anti-cytokine antibody infusions, that are already used for treating the bodily signs and symptoms of inflammation but have not yet been used as treatments for the inflamed mind.

that my new colleagues had reasoned that his panicky symptoms of a racing pulse and over-breathing were caused by his mental state of anxiety, and that he was self-medicating with alcohol in a misguided effort to subdue his anxiety and control his panic attacks. It was all in the mind. I listened to his heart and lungs with my stethoscope and it seemed that the story could be told the other way round. His heavy drinking was causing his heart muscle to fail – it was a case of alcoholic cardiomyopathy, to use the physicianly jargon – and the heart failure was causing his body to pump adrenaline, which was driving his panic and anxiety. It was not all in the mind. These were mental symptoms of a physical disorder.

After a couple of such cases, the consultant psychiatrist I was working for at the time had a quiet word with me. Of course it was a good thing, she said, that I was helping this man and others to find medical treatment. But what did it signify about my attitude to becoming a psychiatrist? Had I fully accepted – or was I in denial – that I was now on a very different career path, which would take me ever further away from the world of the body and ever deeper into the world of the mind? She saw my stethoscope as a kind of comfort blanket, a symptom of *my* anxiety about leaving behind the more prestigious, white-coated company of physicians and becoming a lowly psychiatrist instead. "I think you need to cut the umbilical cord," she said, smiling at me bravely, meaning I had to abandon medical practice if I was to be reborn as a psychiatrist. I didn't think I was in denial; but then, you wouldn't, would you? I quickly realised that if I assertively denied that I was in denial this would be interpreted, from her Freudian perspective, as libidinal reinforcement of my unconscious defence mechanisms, as proof that she was right. I still have my stethoscope, on a shelf in my office, but I haven't used it for about 25 years.

It is just another anecdote, I know, but I don't think my experiences as a medical student, a young physician, or a young psychiatrist, were or are particularly unusual. I see them all as trivial but typical consequences of the Cartesian partition of the human condition into two qualitatively distinct domains, reflected in the rigid demarcation of physical from mental health. The more serious consequence of this medical apartheid, in my opinion, is that it is a bad deal for patients.

We have seen already that apartheid was not a good deal for medical patients, like Mrs P. She was left stranded in no-man's land with her "co-morbid depression". Her physicians didn't see it as their problem. A psychiatrist couldn't call it a bona fide case of MDD. Her fatigue, pessimism and sense of brain fog were not well recognised or treated on either side of the line. Mrs P was effectively left alone to "get over" or "work through" or "worry less about" significant psychological symptoms of her rheumatoid disease. The culture of stigmatisation and shame would have discouraged her from complaining that the medicine wasn't working – she still felt like shit. If she was a good patient, and Mrs P was, she *would* get on with it, readjust, move on, admirably, somehow. Since then, 1989, there has been some improvement in psychological awareness in medical outpatient clinics, but depression, fatigue and cognitive function are not routinely assessed in patients with major inflammatory disorders in the UK. It seems very likely that there are many people with serious inflammatory disorders who have unrecognised and under-treated psychological symptoms. I would be extremely surprised if there aren't other Mrs Ps out there even today, invisible to their Cartesian physicians.

And I think medical apartheid is also a bad deal for psychiatric patients. One of the most shocking healthcare statistics I know is that the average life expectancy of patients with serious mental illness is at least 10 years less than expected.[82] If you've got a long-term disabling mental illness, like MDD or bipolar disorder or schizophrenia, you're likely to die at a much younger age, even if you live in a rich city like London in 2018. To put it another way, the impact of chronic schizophrenia on life expectancy, the lethality of schizophrenia, is about the same as the lethality of cancer: both cause the loss of 10–15 years of life.

Often when I've shared these statistics with people, they've said, yes/but, it must be because of the suicides. It must be that the life of a patient with serious mental illness is reduced, on average, because disorders of the mind can so derange reason that some patients kill themselves, often while they're still young. But that Cartesian reflex is not the right answer. Even if you take out all deaths by suicide, the life expectancy of people with serious mental illness is still cut by a decade.[83] So-called mental patients are dying younger from physical disorders – like diabetes, heart and lung disease. This could be because, in apartheid healthcare systems, schizophrenia and bipolar disorder are treated solely as diseases of the mind, and many patients have unrecognised and under-treated diseases of the body. People with severe mental illness often have difficulties with self-care and with accessing appropriate medical, educational and social services. Some of the commonly used drugs for psychotic symptoms cause weight gain and diabetes. There are many factors in play but the base fact that serious mental illness is as lethal as cancer cannot be written off as a statistical quirk, attributable to the biasing of the data by a few young deaths by suicide among patients with severe depression, bipolar disorder or schizophrenia. Many patients of all ages with serious mental illness also have serious physical illness. Their prospects are critically disadvantaged by having to negotiate health services that are split between mind and body.

Could it be different already?

Let's imagine that you know someone who is depressed, a friend or a family member, and as you've been reading this book you've been wondering how much of this new science of immuno-psychiatry might be relevant to him. Is there anything that could be done differently now, as a result of thinking about his immune system, that could help him to recover from depression?

What would happen to him if he went to his GP in 2018 and asked her if his depression was anything to do with inflammation? What would the doctor be able to do to assess whether his depression really was related to inflammation? And if it was, what then could she do about it? I'm afraid the most likely outcome would be underwhelming, even if his doctor is terrific, open-minded, well-informed, and has plenty of time on her hands.

What could she actually do with him sitting there in front

of her? She could ask him a lot of questions to work out if he had a medical disorder, like Mrs P's rheumatoid disease, that is known to cause severe inflammation. But if the answer to all those questions was negative – he had no known inflammatory disease – that wouldn't mean he wasn't inflamed enough to cause depression. It could be that he's got an inflammatory disease that he doesn't know about because it hasn't yet been diagnosed. Or it could be that he's moderately inflamed because he's overweight, or because he's stressed by looking after his wife with Alzheimer's disease, or because he was badly treated as a child, or because he is elderly, or some combination of these and other common factors that are known to cause inflammation.

His doctor might sigh. The only way to know more is to do a blood test. But what tests for inflammation are realistically affordable and available in general practice? In 2018 in the UK, the choice is limited. His doctor could probably be persuaded to check his full blood count – measuring the number of macrophages, lymphocytes and other white blood cells in circulation – and the blood level of C-reactive protein, or CRP.

Let's say the doctor does a blood test for CRP and the result is 4.8 mg/L. What does it mean? It's not stratospherically high – so it doesn't suggest he's got a major undiagnosed disorder, which is good news. But it's outside the normal range. Most doctors reckon that CRP should be less than 3 mg/L to count as normal, so 4.8 is enough to count as low-grade or moderate inflammation. Your friend or family member would then have more reason to believe that his depression could be related to his bodily inflammation; but what could he or his doctor do differently as a result?

An obvious idea would be to try taking one of the many anti-inflammatory drugs that are already in widespread use, like aspirin. If his depression is caused by inflammation then trying an anti-inflammatory drug makes sense, in principle; but would probably not be recommended by his doctor, in practice. There are two good reasons for current medical reluctance to prescribe anti-inflammatory drugs for patients with inflamed depression. First, there is no solid evidence that aspirin or any other anti-inflammatory drug already in medical use has anti-depressant effects. The clinical trials that would be needed to provide such evidence have simply not been done. There is strong but circumstantial evidence that some anti-inflammatory drugs (minocycline and diclofenac, in particular) have anti-depressant effects when they are prescribed for pain or other inflammatory symptoms.[77] But no anti-inflammatory drugs are officially licensed for treatment of depression. Second, even if your friend's doctor was prepared to prescribe an anti-inflammatory drug "off label" or speculatively, without clear evidence that it was likely to work, she would be deterred by the certain safety risks. Aspirin, for example, commonly causes stomach irritation, ulceration and bleeding. A doctor obedient to the Hippocratic oath to abstain from doing harm to her patients will not prescribe a risky drug in the absence of evidence that the risk is likely to be outweighed by the benefit.

So a careful doctor in 2018 is likely to steer your friend away from existing anti-inflammatory drugs and towards treatment of the underlying cause of his inflammation. And there is a long list of possible reasons for low-grade inflammation to consider, including obesity, age, social stress and seasonal cycles, which I've already mentioned, as well as some that I haven't.

Periodontitis, literally inflammation around the teeth, would be top of my list of culprits if I was inflamed and depressed. This is a low-grade chronic infection that can easily get forgotten because most doctors don't think about it, seeing it as a dentist's business, and most dentists aren't paid to think about the links between gum disease and depression. Does your friend have bad breath? It could be relevant.

Various gastrointestinal disturbances, like irritable bowel syndrome or intermittent colitis, are also likely suspects. The gut is full of bacterial antigens, some of them toxic, and the walls of the gut are eight metres long, about four to five times longer than our average height. All along the watch-towers of this long frontier, between the self and hordes of possibly hostile non-self bacteria, macrophages are concentrated. There are constant skirmishes between invasive gut bacteria and defensive macrophages that pump cytokines into the circulation, and could push up CRP. The inflammatory intensity of so-called leaky gut syndrome is a product of the toxicity of the bacterial flora of the bowel – the microbiome – and the strength of immune response. So someone with a deprived or abused childhood, one can imagine, whose macrophage army is already on yellow alert after exposure to such early and severe social stress, might have a more inflamed and depressed reaction to hostile gut bacteria in the microbiome many years later. It's complicated. Not only are there many individual factors that can each cause low-grade inflammation, they can also interact with each other to compound their inflammatory effects.

If your friend's doctor can help him to find the causes of his low-grade inflammation he could try to tackle them. He could lose weight if he was obese, which would bring down his cytokine levels. He could try a new dentist or changing his diet. A lot of sensible practices, like physical exercise, sleeping well and avoiding excess alcohol, may have anti-inflammatory benefits. But in terms of lifestyle management this is motherhood and apple pie: very good and very familiar advice that is often very hard to follow. And there may be reasons why he is inflamed that are not so amenable to self-help: how can he escape the stress of caring for a loved one without incurring the guilt of not caring for a loved one? What can he do to change what happened to him as a child? Or what is happening to his body as he gets older?

In short, what could your friend do differently? And this is why his doctor might have sighed. She would have seen this coming. None of this immunological detective work about possible causes of depression will immediately make much difference to his treatment. There is some evidence that inflamed patients respond less well to anti-depressant treatment with conventional drugs, like SSRIs. So knowing that his CRP is 4.8, and therefore outside the normal range, might make her think twice about prescribing another SSRI if he's already tried one that didn't work. That's not a very exciting therapeutic advance from your friend's point of view – closing down a treatment option – although conceptually it would be an advance on current practice to use a biomarker like CRP, indeed any biomarker, to predict anti-depressant treatment response. But that's not much upside. The fact of the matter is that there are no anti-depressant treatments, of any sort, that are focused on reducing inflammation. It couldn't be different already. There has been plenty of progress in the scientific theory of how the immune and the nervous systems interact; but this new knowledge is not yet enough to make a difference to the real-life experience of depression. The only thing that really drives change in medical practice is new treatment.

Market failure

In the decades since Prozac's launch in 1989, the pharmaceutical and biotech industries have invested billions of dollars in the search for new treatments for depression. The return on that investment – scientifically, therapeutically, commercially – has been discouraging, to put it mildly. Almost nothing has worked. Many promising leads have been pursued, hundreds of clinical trials have been conducted; but there has been no second wave of anti-depressant innovation to follow the wave that started with the accidental discovery of iproniazid and peaked with the advent of SSRIs.

Acting rationally, companies have stepped back, not wanting to put good money after bad. The level of spending on research and development (R&D) for depression and other mental health disorders has dwindled, projects have been abruptly terminated, scientists have lost their jobs or been reassigned to other therapeutic areas. There are now many fewer new drugs for depression in the R&D pipeline than there were 30 years ago. High levels of investment may not have succeeded in discovering new anti-depressants in the past but it demands gravity-defying optimism to believe that lower levels of investment will be more successful in the future. All other things being equal, less investment will lead to a lower probability of new treatments emerging, and this at a time when depression consistently ranks as one of the single biggest causes of disability among working-age adults worldwide. The level of unmet clinical need could hardly be higher but the level of public and private sector investment is disproportionately low. In an ideal market economy this shouldn't happen. High levels of demand should stimulate high levels of investment in supplying new products that could meet that demand and close the gap in the market. Money and talent should be pouring into depression research, in theory, but in fact they're walking away. An economist might diagnose a case of market failure. Industry people tend to say the old business model is broken.

I witnessed a small piece of this story up close in 2010, when I had been working part-time for GlaxoSmithKline for about five years. One Monday afternoon, I dialled in to an urgently scheduled teleconference to hear the news that GSK was closing its psychiatric research centres in Italy and England, effective immediately. More than 500 people would be made redundant, all ongoing projects would be stopped or spun out into smaller companies, and the Italian site would be sold. We were strategically exiting the whole area of mental health. And GSK wasn't the only big company making that move; a few weeks later, Astra Zeneca announced an equally swingeing cut to its R&D budget for mental health. It isn't too hard to grasp the financial logic of these decisions, or to work out why the model was broken.[84] It was (and is) more challenging to know what to do next.

The broken business model for anti-depressant drug development is the way of working that became customary throughout the industry following the path pioneered by Prozac, from about 1990 to 2010. It started with a drug target in the brain, often serotonin, noradrenaline, dopamine or a related molecule. Then thousands of candidate drugs were screened by robots in the lab for their biochemical potency to bind to the target and change the way it worked in a test tube. Once a few candidate drugs had been prioritised from among the thousands initially considered, they were tested on animals, mainly to investigate their safety, and partly in the hope of seeing early signs of efficacy.

If a mouse is suspended by its tail, so it is hanging upside down in mid-air, it will struggle to get free or reorient itself, for a while; then it will cease struggling and hang quietly. This procedure became known as the tail suspension test and was widely used and described as an animal model of depression for decades, despite its obvious limitations then and now. The principal rationale was that some of the first anti-depressant drugs had sedative side effects, so they made mice struggle less on the tail suspension test, and it was supposed that any new anti-depressant should have similar effects. There was never any convincing demonstration that the mice were depressed, before or after they were suspended upside down. So the industry wasn't exactly using mice to find new anti-depressants; it was using mice to find new drugs that matched the side-effect profile of old anti-depressants. You don't have to be a Cartesian to see that an upside-down mouse is not a great animal model of human depression.

The most promising candidate drugs that made it through this pre-clinical process of chemical screening and animal testing were then tested in humans. Phase 1 trials were conducted in healthy volunteers to confirm that the drug was safe and to identify the maximum tolerated dose. Then came the critical step of phase 2: the first clinical trials of the drug in depressed patients. Like the animal testing procedures, phase 2 studies were often designed formulaically to follow a traditional path. A few hundred patients with MDD were recruited and randomly assigned, usually on a 50/50 split, to treatment with a placebo, or treatment with the new drug, for two or three months. At the start and end of the treatment period, patients were interviewed by a psychiatrist, or completed a self-report questionnaire of their depressive symptoms. If the drug-treated patients reported greater improvement in their symptoms than the placebo-treated patients, then the trial was regarded as a success and the drug could move forward to the third and final phase of clinical testing. Phase 3 followed essentially the same experimental plan as phase 2, but on a bigger scale, with studies typically involving thousands rather than hundreds of patients overall. If the placebo-controlled effect of the drug was still statistically significant at the end of phase 3, the data could be submitted for approval of a marketing licence by a government agency.

The levels of investment increased by roughly an order of magnitude from one million dollars for a study in phase 1, to ten million dollars for a phase 2 study, and 100 million dollars for a phase 3 study. The total cost of getting a molecule all the way to the mental health market was reckoned to be about 850 million dollars in 2010. But most drugs failed somewhere en route. The overall probability of success was less than 10% and the few drugs that made it all the way had to generate enormous amounts of money if they were to recover their own development costs as well as the sunk costs of all the failed trials of less successful candidates. The only happy ending was a commercial blockbuster, a drug that was capable of earning billions of dollars a year, by being prescribed to the largest possible number of depressed people.

Looking back, it is not surprising that this model eventually broke. It seems more remarkable that there was ever a time when it was not broken. Nothing about it now makes sense scientifically. The choice of targets and animal tests was often designed to prioritise product line extensions, or "me too" drugs that were as close as possible to successful precursors. To put it bluntly, the industry kept hammering away at serotonin, dopamine and related targets rather than successfully exploring alternative targets for more innovative drugs. And there was generally a "one size fits all" approach to clinical trials and marketing: an anti-depressant drug was assumed to be equally good for all patients with depression. Not much effort was usually made to understand how a physical agent like a drug could have effects on a mental state like depression. Old-school clinical trials didn't measure biomarkers, or sequence DNA, or look at brain scans. To be fair, not all these biomedical techniques were available in the 1990s and early 2000s. And some of the methods that might have been very useful then, like a brain scan for serotonin levels, are still not available today. But the absence of any biological data from the industry trials contributed to a lack of deep understanding about how the drugs worked or which patients they might work best for: as I later discovered in my Molière moment at the Maudsley Hospital.

The business of the blockbuster model was not too troubled by the philosophical or farcical paradox of an anti-depressant drug in a Cartesian world. If a development programme could leap from the tail suspension test to positive phase 3 data then it was legitimised by its own improbable success. What more do you want? But once the market was crowded by the early winners of this lottery, and commercial success had become increasingly elusive for the "fast followers", it was the model itself that was found wanting. It couldn't explain its failures. It couldn't predict its successes. It was scientifically exhausted and it went out of business. That much was not a market failure; it was the inevitable fate of a business model that has run out of steam and been overtaken by market forces. The same thing happened about 150 years earlier to the once-thriving business of herbal remedies for unbalanced humours.

Economists like to talk about creative destruction – the death of old businesses at the hands of the market creating space for new and better businesses to flourish. Sometimes the old business may be disrupted by an insurgent new business competitor, and sometimes the old business can collapse for other reasons, before a strong competitive business has been marketed. When the old business model for anti-depressant drug discovery collapsed, in 2010, it wasn't because a new business model for depression was ready to replace it. It was simply because the old business model was unsustainable: not enough return on investment; not enough therapeutic innovation to justify the massive development costs.

The old model died before a new model was ready. And there is no law of economics according to which a new model must be born within six months, or six years, or 60 years, of the death of the old model. It could take any amount of time for a company or a sector to reinvest in an area of recent business collapse. The economic destruction may be necessary but it is not always rapidly creative.

A few weeks after that Monday afternoon teleconference, I asked my boss at GSK if he thought the company would ever reinvest in depression and psychiatry. "I'd never say never. But if we were going to go back there," he said, as gravely as if the destination were Chernobyl, "it would have to be completely different. What we're not going to do is stop, wait a bit, and then start doing exactly the same thing we did before all over again. So don't ask me for tens of millions to jump back into old-school phase 2 because that's not going to happen any time soon. First, you've got to be able to tell me how it's going to be different next time."

Beyond blockbusters: better but not bigger than Prozac

There can be no more talk of panaceas. We will need to leave behind the idea that depression is all one thing, in much the same way that we no longer think of cancer as one multi-headed monster disease but as a collection of thousands of different kinds of diseases. We will need to recognise that there could be many different causes of depression and therefore to challenge the possibility of a panacea. How could any single treatment, an SSRI or a course of cognitive behavioural therapy, say, conceivably provide the best possible treatment for all patients, regardless of the many different underlying causes of their depression?

Panaceas are scientifically ruled out. We will have to think instead about how to identify major causes of depression, and how to define groups of depressed patients who share a common cause, and might particularly benefit from a specific treatment. This approach is obviously good from the patient's perspective because it reduces exposure to the risks of treatment for those who are least likely to benefit. Translating the science of neuro-immunology to anti-depressants along these lines, we will need to design treatments that are targeted at inflammatory mechanisms that cause depression in a subset of depressed patients, not necessarily all patients with depression. The expectation is that anti-inflammatory drugs could work well for patients with inflamed depression. There will be other patients with depressive symptoms, who are not inflamed, who are likely to get the most benefit from existing anti-depressant treatments or any new non-immunological treatments that might be developed in future.

Prozac and its cousins were blockbusters in two ways: massive commercial success and virtually unbounded licence. They were used as if they were panaceas, to provide a one-size-fits all treatment for depression (and many other disorders). The next generation of anti-depressant drugs will probably be more personalised products that can offer a major therapeutic benefit to patients who are depressed for a particular reason. The development and launch of new anti-depressant drugs is likely to be coupled to so-called companion diagnostics, biomarkers that are validated and licensed for use in conjunction with the new drug. A simple clinical procedure – perhaps a blood test – will be used to predict which depressed patients are most likely to benefit from the new drug. Could this kind of niche-buster product be commercially successful, on the same scale as an old-school blockbuster anti-depressant like Prozac?

Who knows? But from a commercial perspective, the size of the potential market is obviously an important consideration. How big would the market be for a drug that worked very well as an anti-depressant but only worked for the percentage of patients whose depression was linked to inflammation? That is going to depend on the cut-off criterion used to define which patients are inflamed and which are not. It is also going to depend on whether you're focused only on depression as a mental illness, typified by the conventional psychiatric diagnosis of MDD, or whether you're also prepared to think about co-morbid depression in patients, like Mrs P, who have a physical illness. To get a rough idea, let's start from the fact that about 350 million people, or about 7% of the world's population, had an episode of MDD in 2012. How many of these people would we expect to pass a blood test for inflammation? If we used CRP as the biomarker, and 3 mg/L as the cut-off point for being inflamed, then we might expect about a third of the patients with MDD to be eligible for treatment with a new anti-inflammatory drug. That's more than 100 million people. One of the few good things about there being an enormous number of depressed people in the world is that commercially it creates an opportunity to provide a personalised product, for a biomarker-defined niche in the market, with mass-market economies of scale.

New drug development for inflamed depression will mean validating the blood tests that will be used to decide if depressed patients are eligible for treatment; and then testing the drug in groups of patients that are predicted by the inflammatory biomarker to be responsive (or not responsive) to treatment. This will all take a great deal of time and money to do rigorously to the standards needed for the licensing of a new anti-depressant medicine. In the best case, I think, new anti-inflammatory drugs might become available to patients, like Mrs P, with co-morbid depression about five years from now; and for some patients with MDD about 5–10 years from now. That might seem like a long time. But from a hard-nosed industry perspective the probability of success is still less than 50%. Remember, most drug development projects fail, especially anti-depressant drug development projects, where the percentage of clinical trials reporting positive outcomes has been dismally low at times. If you asked around the pharma and biotech industries now, I think you'd get the overall impression that there might be a 20% chance that anti-inflammatory drugs could really make it all the way as a new class of anti-depressants. Positive new clinical trial results in the next few years could increase that 20% probability of success dramatically. But there have been many false dawns in the history of psychiatry and the recent surge of optimism about immunological anti-depressants could yet prove to be another one: there's still risk in the package, as they say. And there will be until there is convincingly positive clinical trial data – which we haven't yet seen.

Encouraging the industry to move forward into clinical

trials, there are dozens of anti-inflammatory drugs that have already been developed or licensed for other disorders that could potentially be useful for treatment of inflamed depression. The industry jargon for this is repurposing.[85] It makes it possible, in principle, to target a range of immune mechanisms for depression without incurring the costs associated with developing a new anti-inflammatory drug from scratch, from the first biochemical screening studies through testing in animal models to phase 1 safety studies. By allowing companies to go straight to phase 2, repurposing can make it a lot cheaper, less time-consuming and less risky to discover whether a drug that is already known to hit its target safely in the human immune system could be effective in depressed patients.

Despite the radioactive fall-out from the implosion of the old business model that still hangs over depression, the still-fresh memories of huge investment that didn't go according to plan, repurposing could help the industry to start going back there. In the best case, there could be a wave of innovation, based on repurposing some of the hundreds of anti-inflammatory drugs that are already in existence but have not traditionally been regarded as relevant to disorders of the mind. And in the very best case, this could happen relatively quickly, in 5–10 years, say, rather than the 20 years it usually takes to get from a new target, like serotonin circa 1970, to a new medicine, like Prozac circa 1990.

It is also encouraging that there is a virtually limitless number of potential biomarkers that could be used to predict which patients are more likely to respond to anti-inflammatory drugs. I have talked a lot about CRP, but that doesn't mean it is the best or only biomarker for inflamed depression. It simply reflects the fact that CRP has been around for a long time in medicine, it was readily available to use in the first immuno-psychiatry studies in the 1990s and it has since served as a leading light in an originally obscure area. But I would expect there to be better biomarkers out there: tests that are capable of showing greater differences between groups of patients, or that are more precisely related to the mechanism of action of a new drug, than blood levels of CRP or cytokines. Modern immunology boasts an extraordinary range of techniques for profiling the peripheral immune system, many of which are only just beginning to find their way into depression research. CRP has already proven to be the first useful immune biomarker for depression; it certainly won't be the last, or the best for all purposes.

We can also be encouraged, to some degree, by looking back at old clinical trial data through a new lens. In the last 10 years, following the pioneering lead of anti-TNF (tumour necrosis factor) antibodies for treatment of rheumatoid arthritis, dozens of anti-cytokine antibodies have been tested in trials for many different inflammatory disorders. As you'd expect, all the anti-cytokine antibody trials published to date have been designed according to an experimental plan or protocol that prioritises measurement of the drug's effect on the patient's physical health. Most of the studies of new antibodies for rheumatoid arthritis, for example, have used physical examination of swollen joints as the primary endpoint, the key measure of whether the drug works, and whether the trial will be regarded as a success. Mental health has not been entirely neglected in these clinical trials for physical health disorders. It has often been measured, if cursorily, as a secondary endpoint, using questionnaires that simply ask patients, on a scale of 1 to 4: How depressed are you feeling? How much energy do you have? So, it is possible to reanalyse these secondary endpoints, these mental health scores, as the principal outcome of the study, as if the studies had been designed to test the drug effects on depression (rather than joint swelling in arthritis). And the results are apparently impressive. Recent studies that have reanalysed mental health data from dozens of placebo-controlled trials on tens of thousands of patients with various disorders, including rheumatoid arthritis, psoriasis and asthma,[86–88] have shown that the anti-inflammatory drugs tested had an anti-depressant effect size of about 0.4, on average. How big a deal is that? 0.4 might not look like a big number but bear in mind that the average effect of SSRIs is only about 0.2 on the same scale. On the face of it, new anti-inflammatory drugs could be twice as effective at treating symptoms of depression as currently standard anti-depressant drugs.

But there's a catch. It's another version of the same old Cartesian catch. In all the clinical trials conducted so far, the drug effects on depression have not been measured for the first time until about two or three months after the start of treatment. By then, many patients will have experienced significant improvements in their physical health. Arthritic patients will have less painful joints and better looking X-rays of their joints; psoriatic patients will have fewer and smaller plaques of inflamed red skin on their faces and elbows. And as any Cartesian will be quick to point out, if you thought you had an incurable disease, then you tried a new treatment that cured it, you would feel a lot less depressed, wouldn't you? The anti-depressant effects of anti-cytokine treatment are superficially visible but deeply discounted by the same line of reasoning that licenses medical indifference to the mental health symptoms of inflammatory disease.

It comes back to the question of causality. To show that anti-inflammatory drugs can directly cause an improvement in mental health, rather than a mental reaction to improved physical health, we need to see that the beneficial effects on mental health precede or anticipate any later effects on physical health. The under-investigated Remicade high – the rapid boost in mood that many patients report soon after their first dose of an anti-TNF antibody – indicates that anti-inflammatory drugs could have such rapid anti-depressant effects. And, of course, it would be very useful for doctors and patients to have access to anti-depressant drugs that worked more rapidly than the two to six weeks usually required for SSRIs to work. But we will have to do the studies.

So far there have been very few placebo-controlled clinical trials deliberately designed to test the anti-depressant effects of anti-inflammatory drugs, and their results are not conclusive. Only one study has been reported of an anti-cytokine antibody.[89] Sixty patients with treatment-resistant depression, who had not responded well to conventional anti-depressant drugs, were randomly assigned to treatment with an anti-TNF antibody or a placebo. After eight weeks, the group of patients treated with the antibody reported substantial improvement in the severity of their depressive symptoms; but so too did the patients treated with a placebo. There was no significant difference, on average, between the two groups.

In that sense, the trial was negative.

But when the investigators dug a bit deeper into the data, they found that not all patients responded to treatment in the same way. The patients who had higher levels of CRP at baseline, before the start of the trial, had a stronger anti-depressant response to treatment than the patients who had lower levels. In other words, the anti-inflammatory drug was not a panacea: it seemed to work better for depressed patients who were inflamed than it did for depressed patients who were not. In that sense, the trial was positive.

It points to a future in which trials for an anti-inflammatory drug for depression will routinely use an inflammatory biomarker up front to identify those depressed patients that are most likely to benefit from treatment. Despite the inherent risks in any drug development project, I think there will be significant investment in this new kind of anti-depressant drug trial in the immediate future. And it will certainly be interesting to watch this space over the next few years.

But what about non-drug treatments for inflamed depression? Are there any other ways, besides drugs, that we can break the vicious cycle that links stress, inflammation and depression?

We know from the recent discovery of the inflammatory reflex that the vagus nerve controls cytokine release by macrophages in the spleen. We also know that vagal nerve stimulation by an electrical device implanted in the body can dramatically reduce inflammation and improve symptoms in patients with rheumatoid arthritis. What is not widely known is that vagal nerve stimulation has been licensed for treatment of depression since 2005.

Many depressed patients have had stimulating electrodes implanted close to the vagus nerve as it travels down the neck, with a control device just under the skin so the patient can adjust the timing and duration of vagal stimulation. This procedure was licensed because it is safe and apparently efficacious. It seems to work, although most of the studies have not controlled for a placebo effect, so it has questionable added value. And, if it works, it is still not clear how it works.[90] The traditional explanation, which is not strongly supported by experimental data, is that the electrical stimuli from the device travel up the vagus nerve to the brain stem, where they activate the cells that manufacture serotonin and noradrenaline, and this increases serotonin signalling to the rest of the brain. In other words, vagal nerve stimulation has been thought to work like an electrical SSRI. But maybe it works more like an electrical anti-cytokine antibody? It may be that the anti-depressant effect depends on the electrical stimulation passing down the vagus to the spleen, not up the vagus to the brain, and is explained by reduced inflammatory cytokines in the body, not by increased serotonin in the brain. We don't know right now.

If it became clearer that vagal nerve stimulation worked for depression via its anti-inflammatory effects, this could open the door to using blood biomarkers to predict which patients are most likely to benefit from having an expensive stimulator surgically implanted. And it might foster further research to develop smarter, less invasive ways of implanting stimulators and delivering electrical stimuli to the vagus nerve. The technology of bio-electronics – devices for electrical monitoring and stimulation of biological processes – is moving rapidly, but not yet in the direction of new treatments for depression. It is conceivable that this could change and in the next 10 years or so we might see a new generation of bio-electronic devices appear that can electrically subdue the inflammatory signals that drive depression.[91]

We also know, from the recent discoveries about stress-related inflammation, that social and psychological shocks, like public speaking or an abusive relationship, can increase bodily inflammation. That might make you think that a course of psychotherapy or meditation, focused on helping patients to strengthen skills for stress management, could have anti-inflammatory effects. And indeed there is some evidence for this. Mindfulness training reduced loneliness in older adults and also reduced expression of inflammatory genes by white blood cells.[92] A recent combined analysis of the results of multiple studies of the immunological effects of mind-body therapies, like meditation or tai chi, found that they significantly reduced the expression of genes that control activation of macrophages in response to infection.[93] It seems that the mind can be trained to control the inflammatory response of the body, and this might be one of the mechanisms by which psychological treatments are effective for depression.

It might not be so obvious how this neuro-immunological explanation could change psychological treatment for depression, since meditation and other stress management techniques are already moderately effective and widely used. But perhaps there is an opportunity for inflammatory markers to be used as a kind of biofeedback, providing detailed information on how bodily inflammation is progressively controlled as people practise meditation and develop stress management skills. You could call it cytokine-guided psychotherapy. As far as I know it hasn't happened yet. But there is no fundamental reason, in a post-Cartesian world, why the effects of psychological treatment should be restricted to the mind or why it wouldn't make sense to try measuring the effects of meditation on macrophages.

Alzheimer's disease and the yin and yang of microglia

Although dementia sounds like an ancient word, as old as melancholia or inflammation, it wasn't invented until the 18th century, when a couple of Latin words were jammed together to create a new one meaning loss of mind. It was only at the end of the 19th century that it began to occur to the first generations of neuroscientists that dementia could be caused by a brain disease rather than by *anno domini*, the passing of mortal time. The late 19th-century scientist Alois Alzheimer now has name recognition on a par with Freud, and is hugely more famous than his contemporary and mentor Emil Kraepelin, but he wasn't a towering figure in his own lifetime. His claim to fame rests on a single case, a woman in her fifties called Auguste Deter, one of his patients in an asylum near Frankfurt, who had a rapidly progressive dementia despite being far from senile.[94] When she died, at the age of 56, Alzheimer arranged for her brain to be sent to the anatomy lab he had just been invited to set up in Kraepelin's new Institute for Brain and Mental Health in

Munich. Alzheimer looked down the microscope at pieces of her brain and noticed that there were unusual fibres and clumps of stained material in and around the nerve cells. They were what we now call plaques and tangles. Alzheimer described them clearly enough for us to be sure that's what he saw; but his colleagues weren't immediately impressed.

The story goes that at a psychiatric conference in 1907, where Alzheimer first presented his findings, his lecture was immediately followed by a more keenly awaited presentation of a case of compulsive masturbation, and he faced no questions from the audience. I said earlier that it is stressful to be asked questions in public; and it is, but for a scientist it is also humiliating to be asked no questions at all at the end of a lecture. It implies that nothing you have said has been interesting enough even to excite scepticism. Frau Deter's brain plaques and tangles might have slipped below the surface of history for ever if not for Kraepelin, who remembered them and relaunched her as the world's first case of Alzheimer's disease in the eighth edition of his textbook on psychiatry in 1910.

Kraepelin considered Alzheimer's disease to be a rare cause of dementia that occurred in a few, younger people like Frau D, but was not the cause of the much commoner senile dementia, which was attributed to a reduced blood supply to the brain. That is roughly what we were still being taught about dementia as medical students at Bart's in the 1980s: and "crumble" was what we called it under our breath. It is only in the last 25 years or so, since ex-President Ronald Reagan disclosed his diagnosis in 1994, that Alzheimer's name has become known to us all. We have realised that the majority of cases of dementia in our ageing societies are due to his disease, the accumulation of plaques and tangles in the brain.

Alzheimer had no idea what the plaques and tangles were. He described them simply as "a peculiar material". It has since been discovered that they are formed from proteins, abnormally large quantities of abnormally insoluble proteins, called tau and amyloid. As we get older, all of us will form plaques and tangles of these aggregated and mis-folded proteins in our brains, to some extent; but we won't all "get Alzheimer's". We don't know why plaques and tangles cause a progressive dementia in some people and not in others, but one plausible explanation hinges on the immune system. Tau and amyloid are human proteins, but they are not normal human proteins. From the point of view of the immune system they are antigenic, non-self, alien proteins; and, as you'd expect, they trigger an inflammatory reaction. The microglia, the robocops of the brain, swarm around amyloid plaques, attacking, eating and trying to digest the "peculiarly impregnable" protein they contain. As you might also expect, microglial activation in response to plaques causes collateral damage; nerve cells are damaged or killed by the toxic effects of inflammation in the brain. In fact, it seems that the secondary, inflammatory reaction of the microglia could be a more potent cause of death of nerve cells, and therefore a more powerful driver of progressive loss of memory and other cognitive functions, than the primary problem of plaques and tangles.

If it is true that dementia is determined as much by the immune response to Alzheimer's "peculiar material" as by the plaques and tangles themselves, then anti-inflammatory treatments should be effective in slowing or preventing the progression of Alzheimer's disease. There is some evidence in support of this prediction, but so far only some.[95]

Patients like Mrs P, who must take anti-inflammatory drugs on a regular basis to control symptoms of arthritis or other immune disorders of the body, have significantly reduced rates of Alzheimer's disease.[96] Conversely, untreated infection or inflammation in the body is recognised to increase the risk of Alzheimer's disease and to accelerate the rate of progression of dementia.[58] The inflammatory cytokines pumped into the circulation by macrophages dealing with a chronic infection like periodontitis, say, can get across the blood–brain barrier (BBB) and activate microglia, making them more likely to respond aggressively to amyloid plaques and increasing the collateral damage to nerve cells. That's one reason why I keep going to the dentist, even though it makes me depressed in the short term. I figure that any steps I can reasonably take to calm down inflammation in my gums and teeth are likely to be beneficial to my ageing brain in the long term.

However, clinical trials of anti-inflammatory drugs for Alzheimer's have not yet produced a clear winner. As usual with failed trials, there is some disagreement about the reasons why. It is unlikely that all the drugs that have been tested have been given at a high enough dose, or have been able to get across the BBB into the brain. More radically, some scientists have made the important counter-argument that not all microglial activity is bad. The microglial cells, after all, are trying to do the right thing. They are trying to eliminate plaques from the aged brain, and under the microscope you can sometimes see them stuffed full of amyloid protein that they have eaten and are struggling to digest. There is a reasonable case that, therapeutically, we should be trying to support and assist the good work that microglia are doing, not trying to shut them down. That is the rationale for the development of anti-amyloid antibodies that can get into the patient's brain and bind to plaques, making it easier for microglia to identify and destroy them. It is also the rationale for the development of vaccines against Alzheimer's, which involve injecting healthy people with fragments of amyloid to stimulate the production of antibodies that could help microglia deal with amyloid plaques when they begin to form in later life. However, to date, none of the new antibodies or vaccines designed to assist "good" microglia have been more effective than any of the anti-inflammatory drugs designed to inhibit "bad" microglia.

Personally, I suspect that the most likely root cause for the lack of progress in Alzheimer's is the same as for the lack of progress in depression: the curse of the blockbuster. Although it was originally described as a single case, and then regarded as exceedingly rare for about 80 years, it has turned out to be unfortunately common. Alzheimer's disease is now recognised as a major public health and economic challenge, especially in the more rapidly ageing rich countries. As life expectancy improves in poor countries, and more people live into their sixties and beyond, it is predictable that the incidence and impact of Alzheimer's disease will escalate in developing economies. It is a global disorder. And most global disorders, like depression, obesity, high blood pressure, diabetes, atherosclerosis, etc, have multiple causes.

Alzheimer's disease is no exception. There isn't one gene for Alzheimer's; there never was and there never will be. There are many genes that can increase risk of Alzheimer's, most of them having only modest effects, but collectively acting across a range of biochemical pathways in the brain. And the long process of cognitive decline over decades, the clinical syndrome of progressive dementia, isn't necessarily driven by the same biological mechanisms all the way.

Once again, we shouldn't be thinking about it as if it were one thing. We shouldn't be trying to find a panacea. We should be targeting treatments more precisely at those patients most likely to respond. In that sense, the strategy for developing immune treatments for Alzheimer's is exactly the same as the high-level strategy for inflamed depression. Use biomarkers to identify the subgroups of patients that are most (and least) likely to respond to treatment in clinical trials. The genetic profile of patients with Alzheimer's disease is one possible biomarker that could be developed to predict response to anti-inflammatory drugs. For example, one of the genes that has recently been discovered to increase risk for Alzheimer's disease, called *TREM2*, is important for controlling the activity of the microglia in the brain.[97] It may be that dementia in patients with a risky *TREM2* mutation is caused or accelerated by an abnormal state of microglial inflammation. And it is conceivable that this *TREM2*-positive group of patients, or other Alzheimer's patients with clear inflammatory risk factors, would be most likely to benefit from anti-inflammatory treatment.

Alzheimer's isn't one thing and the brain's innate immune system is at least two things, yin and yang, protective and self-destructive. This is not classic blockbuster territory. It's never going to be one size fits all, therapeutically, but you sense there could be some good opportunities to develop personalised immune treatments for Alzheimer's disease in the next 5–10 years.

Schizophrenia and auto-intoxication

As a new consultant psychiatrist in Cambridge, in 1999, I was one of a team of doctors, nurses and psychologists that set up a clinical service for patients who were experiencing their first symptoms of psychosis. They had heard voices or seen things that weren't really there: hallucinations. And/or they believed things that weren't really true: delusions. Hallucinations and delusions are the diagnostic hallmarks of psychosis – or madness – and have been since the ancients.

We used to see young people, mostly in their late teens or early twenties, who had just become psychotic, and try to work out why that might have happened and what we could do about it. No two patients were the same. No two families were the same. We saw straight-arrow undergraduates from Cambridge colleges as well as the alumni of children's homes and juvenile detention centres. Their psychotic symptoms were mixed in with variable amounts of anxiety and depression, sometimes with manic euphoria. Sometimes the timing of psychotic symptoms was related to a possibly causal event, like smoking a lot of cannabis at a party, or getting evicted from housing to sleep on the street. Sometimes the psychosis came out of the blue, abruptly, or emerged so gradually that it was difficult to say when it had begun. Sometimes the standard treatments worked well, sometimes they didn't. Overall, I would say that most patients benefited at least as much from their supportive human contacts with the team as they did from the drugs. But there was one dark question that was always in the back of everyone's mind. "Am I going mad?" "Is my daughter going mad?" "Is this just the start, the first episode, of a relentless march to down-and-out madness that will blight the rest of our lives?" The diagnosis that everyone dreaded, the word that nobody wanted to say, was schizophrenia.

It's a word that's been badly abused and widely misunderstood. It is yet another Greek neologism, meaning split mind, that was coined in the early 20th century by one of Freud's early followers, who thought that psychosis was all in the mind. Schizophrenia and schizophrenic are now often bandied about in conversation to mean things like split personality, or conflicted, or indecisive, or dangerous, or even politically rivalrous. But what schizophrenia means in psychiatry is much closer to the vision of Emil Kraepelin, who described for the first time the trajectory that our patients and their parents most feared. Kraepelin was not a solitary genius like Freud, Ramón y Cajal, Paracelsus or Descartes. He was an organiser, a systematiser, a manager and an encyclopaedist. He raised funds from Jewish families to build a psychiatric hospital and research institute in Munich – one of the very first buildings to bring neuroscience close to treatment for serious mental illness. He worked with or trained many of the leading figures of German-speaking psychiatry and brain science in the first half of the 20th century, which was in many ways a golden era. Most influentially, he produced 11 editions of his compendious textbook,[98] between 1883 and 1925, the year before his death.

Kraepelin marshalled an enormous quantity of clinical observations in support of a simple scheme: psychosis represented one of two possible underlying disease processes – manic-depressive insanity or dementia praecox. One of the key differences between them was their evolution over time, their natural history. Patients with manic depression were expected to swing up and down, perhaps extremely enough to lose touch with reason, but to return to equilibrium between excursions. The trajectory was bumpy in the short term but flat in the long term. Whereas patients with dementia praecox, or precocious dementia in English, suffered a more relentless and progressive course in Kraepelin's book. He called it "sub-acute development of a peculiar simple condition of mental weakness occurring at a youthful age". Young people were becoming demented by madness, progressively less capable and independent, doomed to years on the back wards of large asylums.

Although no one, not even Kraepelin, has ever been entirely convinced that psychosis can be so simply and cleanly divided in two, this formulation is still embedded in the current *DSM* diagnostic system for psychiatry. The words have changed. Manic-depressive insanity is now bipolar disorder. And dementia praecox has turned into the word that the families of our patients never wanted to talk about.

Kraepelin was highly critical of Freud and the thriving psychoanalytic movement he had inspired. In Kraepelin's view, the cause of psychosis, especially the type of psychosis we now call schizophrenia, must be physical, not psychological. He stayed on the same side of the Cartesian divide all his life. He didn't switch tracks like Freud, from the neuroscience lab to the couch. His institute conducted many post mortem examinations of brains from schizophrenic patients but there was no equivalent of Auguste Deter among them. Unlike Alzheimer, working down the hall on Frau D's brain, Kraepelin never found anything as distinctively peculiar as plaques or tangles in the schizophrenic brains. He recognised that schizophrenia tended to run in families, suggesting that it was genetically heritable, but he had no way of knowing which genes were involved. He proposed that society might wish to rid itself of the inherited risk for schizophrenia, idiocy and other brain disorders by a eugenic programme of controlled breeding. He died before the Nazi party came to power, but some of his ideas fatally outlived him, staining his reputation to this day.

At the end of his life he still didn't know what caused schizophrenia. He knew it had to come from the body, not the mind, but where in the body? As he struggled with later revisions of his textbook, he was increasingly preoccupied by an idea that somehow never made it into the *DSM*'s diagnostic criteria for schizophrenia 60 years later: the idea that schizophrenia is a whole-body disease, caused by an auto-intoxication or self-poisoning of the brain by the body. Kraepelin's auto-intoxication theory sounds superficially auto-immune – the body mistakenly attacking the self – but in the early 20th century much less was known about the immune system than about the body's hormonal system. Kraepelin's suspicions were focused on the sex glands, not the lymph glands, as the most likely culprit, the most likely source of a bodily poison that attacked the brain and mind. For many years, he tried "organotherapy", injecting testicular or other glandular tissue into patients for treatment of schizophrenia, without any benefit.[99]

It has taken a long time but we now know that Kraepelin was right about at least one big thing: there are genetic causes for schizophrenia. When the human genome was sequenced, in 2000, there was a massive surge of optimism that we would soon be able to find the genes for schizophrenia, as well as for everything else. But only in the last few years have enough DNA data been collected from 37,000 patients to provide a definitive result.[100] We now know that there are approximately 320 genes that increase risk of schizophrenia. The single most strongly associated gene is located in a part of the human genome that is known to be important for the immune system and auto-immunity. This gene, called complement component 4 (C4), produces an inflammatory protein. Different people can have different versions of the C4 gene, and produce slightly different versions of the complement protein. Risk for schizophrenia is significantly increased in people who have the genetic variant associated with increased inflammatory signalling and the same genetic mutation causes damage to the synaptic connections between nerve cells in mice.[101] It is a stunning series of discoveries to go from no genes, to 320 genes, to understanding that the single biggest genetic risk for schizophrenia is mediated by the immune system. But C4 is still only one of hundreds of risk genes, and the cumulative effect of all known genes is modest. There must be other factors at work.

One of the stubborn facts we have known about schizo-phrenia for many years is that your risk is increased if you were born in the winter months.[102] I remember hearing epidemiologists earnestly discuss this result in the mid-1990s and thinking they must be nuts. It must be some kind of blip in the data. How could season of birth have anything to do with someone developing schizophrenia 19 or 25 years later? Unless it was under the baleful influence of Sagittarius? Fortunately, I didn't raise my hand to make these penetrating remarks in public at the time. There is strong evidence that winter births are riskier because there is a higher risk of infec-tion in winter. The mother, the fetus in the last months of pregnancy and the new-born baby, are all at increased risk of infection in the winter months. And it has been found that maternal, fetal and neonatal infections are all associated with greater risk for schizophrenia. In experiments with rats and mice, the infection of the mother or the fetus with viruses can cause long-term changes in the development of the nervous system. And the extent to which a virus impacts on devel-opment of an animal's brain is conditioned by the way its immune system reacts to the viral infection. So it is possible that something similar happens in humans. Genes control-ling the immune system may predispose babies to react to a common viral infection in a way that somehow derails or diverts the future development of the brain and increases the risk for schizophrenia.[103]

It would be an extraordinary step forward to understand these exciting new ideas in more detail, to penetrate the awful murk that still envelops the provenance of schizophrenia. But can neuro-immunology do more than that, more than help us to understand schizophrenia in a new way? Can it help us deliver any new treatments that could make a real difference? Here the situation is less advanced than for either depression or Alzheimer's disease. Fewer trials have been done and fewer drugs have been studied. But there are already some interesting leads to follow. For example, we know that psychotic symptoms that look like schizophrenia can occur in patients who have high levels of an auto-antibody that binds to one of the brain's key neurotransmitter receptors, called NMDA. Like all auto-antibodies, this one is mistakenly produced by the patient's immune system to target one of the patient's own proteins. It is friendly fire, in this case directed against a synaptic receptor that was already known to play a crucial role in psychosis. About eight years ago, some of my old colleagues on the psychosis team at Cambridgeshire & Peterborough NHS Trust decided to measure the levels of this anti-NMDA antibody in the patients they were seeing. In the first 43 patients they tested, four had high levels of auto-antibody.[104] And when they treated a few of the test-positive patients immunologically, to reduce the levels of auto-antibodies in circulation, they found that it made an immediate and lasting difference to their psychotic symptoms. It's not a cure; or even a controlled trial (that's now ongoing); and of course it will not be a panacea (only about 5% of psychosis patients have anti-NMDA auto-antibodies). But it is another reason to be cheerful about how new immunological treatments could be developed in another area of psychiatry where therapeutic progress has stalled in the last 30 years.

So what? So, maybe, in the next five, 10, 20 years we'll see accelerated progress in the development of a radical new approach to treatment of depression and other psychiatric disorders.

Maybe we'll see new drugs that, unlike the old drugs, are not vaguely supposed to work equally well for everyone with depression but are scientifically predicted to work particularly well for some people.

New blood tests to measure the genetic and inflammatory biomarkers that can predict which kind of treatments are likely to work best for which patients.

New clinics that can offer depressed people a more integrated, holistic assessment of their mental and physical health, as if each of them was being individually treated as one patient, not two.

A new breed of doctors more confident about working on both sides of the traditional line between medicine and psychiatry.

A gradual shift away from the culture of apartheid and stigmatisation that compounds the pain of an illness when it is regarded as all in the mind.

So maybe we'll start winning a few more battles in the fight against the biggest health challenges of the 21st century.

We could be on the cusp of a revolution. It won't be televised. And I might be wrong. But I think it has already begun.

References

Chapter 1

1. Mental Health Foundation. *Fundamental Facts About Mental Health.* 2015.
2. Farmer P, Stevenson D. *Thriving at Work.* UK Government; 2017.
3. Dantzer R, O'Connor JC, Freund GG, Johnson RW, Kelley KW. From inflammation to sickness and depression: when the immune system subjugates the brain. *Nature Reviews Neuroscience.* 2008;9:46–56.
4. Raison CL, Capuron L, Miller AH. Cytokines sing the blues: inflammation and the pathogenesis of depression. *Trends in Immunology.* 2006;27:24–31.
5. Smith RS. The macrophage theory of depression. *Medical Hypotheses.* 1991;35:298–306.
6. Maes M. Evidence for an immune response in major depression: A review and hypothesis. *Progress in Neuropsychopharmacology and Biological Psychiatry.* 1995;19:11–38.
7. Khandaker GM, Pearson RM, Zammit S, Lewis G, Jones PB. Association of serum interleukin 6 and C-reactive protein in childhood with depression and psychosis in young adult life: a population-based longitudinal study. *JAMA Psychiatry.* 2014;71:1121–1128.
8. Harrison N, Brydon L, Walker C, Gray M, Steptoe A, Critchley H. Inflammation causes mood changes through alterations in subgenual cingulate activity and mesolimbic connectivity. *Biological Psychiatry.* 2009;66:407–414.
9. Miller AH, Raison CL. The role of inflammation in depression: from evolutionary imperative to modern treatment target. *Nature Reviews Immunology.* 2016;16:22–34.
10. Anders S, Tanaka M, Kinney DK. Depression as an evolutionary strategy for defense against infection. *Brain, Behavior, and Immunity.* 2013;31:9–22.
11. Watson JD, Crick FH. Molecular structure of nucleic acids. *Nature.* 1953;171:737–738.
12. Clinton WJ. The Human Genome Project. 2000; https://www.youtube.com/watch?v=slRyGLmt3qc.
13. Pittenger C, Duman RS. Stress, depression, and neuroplasticity: a convergence of mechanisms. *Neuropsychopharmacology.* 2008;33:88–109.

14. Slavich GM, Irwin MR. From stress to inflammation and major depressive disorder: a social signal transduction theory of depression. *Psychological Bulletin.* 2014;140:774–815.

15. Danese A, Moffitt TE, Harrington H, et al. Adverse childhood experiences and adult risk factors for age-related disease: Depression, inflammation and clustering of metabolic risk markers. *Archives of Pediatric and Adolescent Medicine.* 2009;163:1135–1143.

Chapter 2

16. MacPherson G, Austyn J. *Exploring Immunology: Concepts and evidence.* Germany: Wiley-Blackwell; 2012.

Chapter 3

17. National Rheumatoid Arthritis Society. *Invisible disease: rheumatoid arthritis and chronic fatigue.* London; 2014.

18. Lokhorst G-J. Descartes and the pineal gland. *The Stanford Enyclopedia of Philosophy* 2016; https://plato.stanford.edu/archives/sum2016/entries/pineal-gland/.

19. Descartes R. *Treatise of Man.* Harvard University Press; 1637.

20. Depression Alliance. *Twice as likely: putting long term conditions and depression on the agenda.* London; 2012.

21. Feldmann M. Development of anti-TNF therapy for rheumatoid arthritis. *Nature Reviews Immunology.* 2002;2:364–371.

22. Elliott MJ, Maini RN, Feldmann M, et al. Randomised double-blind comparison of chimeric monoclonal antibody to tumour necrosis factor α (cA2) versus placebo in rheumatoid arthritis. *The Lancet.* 1994;344:1105–1110.

23. Hess A, Axmann R, Rech J, et al. Blockade of TNF-alpha rapidly inhibits pain responses in the central nervous system. *Proceedings of the National Academy of Scientists USA.* 2011;108:3731–3736.

Chapter 4

24. Telles-Correia D, Marques JG. Melancholia before the twentieth century: fear and sorrow or partial insanity? *Frontiers in Psychology.* 2015;6.

25. American Psychiatric Association. *Diagnostic and Statistical Manual of Mental Disorders.* 5th edition ed. Arlington: American Psychiatric Publishing; 2013.

26. Auden WH. In memory of Sigmund Freud. *Another Time.* London: Random House; 1940.

27. Freud S. An autobiographical study. In: Strachey J, ed. *Standard Edition*

of the Complete Psychological Works of Sigmund Freud. Vol 20. London: Hogarth Press; 1927, 1959:1–74.

28. Masson JM. *The Assault on Truth*. New York: Farrar Straus Giroux; 1984.

29. Freud S. Project for a scientific psychology. In: Strachey J, ed. *Standard Edition of the Complete Psychological Works of Sigmund Freud*. Vol 1. London: Hogarth Press; 1895, 1950.

30. Wampold BE, Mondin GW, Moody M, Stich F, Benson K, Ahn H-N. A meta-analysis of outcome studies comparing bona fide psychotherapies: empirically, "all must have prizes". *Psycholological Bulletin*. 1997;122:203–215.

31. Molière. *Le malade imaginaire*. London: Methuen; 1981.

32. Lòpez-Muñoz F, Alamo C. Monoaminergic neurotransmission: the history of the discovery of anti-depressants from 1950s until today. *Current Pharmaceutical Design*. 2009;15:1563–1586.

33. Kline NS. Iproniziad for the treatment of severe depression. *Albert Lasker Clinical Medical Research Award Citations* 1964; http://www.laskerfoundation.org/awards/show/iproniazid-for-the-treatment-of-severe-depression/.

34. Schildkraut JJ. The catecholamine hypothesis of affective disorders: a review of supporting evidence. *American Journal of Psychiatry*. 1965;122:509–522.

35. Wong DT, Perry KW, Bymaster FP. The discovery of fluoxetine hydrochloride (Prozac). *Nature Reviews Drug Discovery*. 2005;4:764–774.

36. Wurtzel E. *Prozac Nation: Young and Depressed in America*. Vancouver: Penguin; 1994.

37. Coles AJ, Twyman CL, Arnold DL, et al. Alemtuzumab for patients with relapsing multiple sclerosis after disease-modifying therapy: a randomised controlled phase 3 trial. *The Lancet*. 2012;380:1829–1839.

38. Bentley B, Branicky R, Barnes CL, et al. The multilayer connectome of *Caenorhabditis elegans*. *PLoS Computational Biology*. 2016;12:p. e1005283.

39. Kapur S, Phillips AG, Insel TR. Why has it taken so long for biological psychiatry to develop clinical tests and what to do about it? *Molecular Psychiatry*. 2012;17:1174–1179.

40. Cavanagh J, Patterson J, Pimlott S, et al. Serotonin transporter residual availability during long-term antidepressant therapy does not differentiate responder and nonresponder unipolar patients. *Biological Psychiatry*. 2006;59:301–308.

Chapter 5

41. Dantzer R, Kelley KW. Stress and immunity: an integrated view of relationships between the brain and the immune system. *Life Sciences.* 1989;44:1995–2008.

42. Haapakoski R, Mathieu J, Ebmeier KP, Alenius H, Kivimaki M. Cumulative meta-analysis of interleukins 6 and 1-beta, tumour necrosis factor-alpha and C-reactive protein in patients with major depressive disorder. *Brain, Behavior, and Immunity.* 2015;49:206–215.

43. Dowlati Y, Herrmann N, Swardfager W, et al. A meta-analysis of cytokines in major depression. *Biological Psychiatry.* 2010;67:446–457.

44. Wium-Andersen MK, Orsted DD, Nielsen SF, Nordestgaard BG. Elevated C-reactive protein levels, psychological distress, and depression in 73,131 individuals. *JAMA Psychiatry.* 2013;70:176–184.

45. Bell JA, Kivimäki M, Bullmore ET, Steptoe A, Carvalho LA, Consortium MI. Repeated exposure to systemic inflammation and risk of new depressive symptoms among older adults. *Translational Psychiatry.* 2017;7:p.e1208.

46. McDonald EM, Mann AH, Thomas HC. Interferons as mediators of psychiatric morbidity: An investigation in a trial of recombinant alpha-interferon in hepatitis B carriers. *The Lancet.* 1987;330:1175–1178.

47. Bull SJ, Huezo-Diaz P, Binder EB, et al. Functional polymorphisms in the interleukin-6 and serotonin transporter genes, and depression and fatigue induced by interferon-α and ribavirin treatment. *Molecular Psychiatry.* 2009;14:1095–1104.

48. Conan Doyle A. *A Study in Scarlet.* Ware: Wordsworth Press; 1887, 2001.

49. Willans G, Searle R. *Down with Skool!* London: Methuen; 1953.

50. Louveau A, Smirnov I, Keyes TJ, et al. Structural and functional features of central nervous system lymphatic vessels. *Nature.* 2015;523:337–341.

51. Galea I, Bechmann I, Perry VH. What is immune privilege (not)? *Trends in Immunology.* 2007;28:12–18.

52. Tracey KJ. The inflammatory reflex. *Nature.* 2002;420:853–859.

53. Koopman FA, Chavan SS, Miljko S, et al. Vagus nerve stimulation inhibits cytokine production and attenuates disease severity in rheumatoid arthritis. *Proceedings of the National Academy of Sciences.* 2016;113:8284–8289.

54. Hamilton JP, Etkin A, Furman DJ, Lemus MG, Johnson RF, Gotlib IH. Functional neuroimaging of major depressive disorder: a meta-analysis and new integration of baseline activation and neural response data. *American Journal of Psychiatry.* 2012;169:693–703.

55. Phan KL, Wager T, Taylor SF, Liberzon I. Functional neuroanatomy of

emotion: a meta-analysis of emotion activation studies in PET and fMRI. *NeuroImage*. 2002;16:331–348.

56. Fu CH, Williams SC, Cleare AJ, et al. Attenuation of the neural response to sad faces in major depression by antidepressant treatment: a prospective, event-related functional magnetic resonance imaging study. *Archives of General Psychiatry*. 2004;61:877–889.

57. Dantzer R, Kelley KW. Twenty years of research on cytokine-induced sickness behavior. *Brain, Behavior, and Immunity*. 2007;21:153–160.

58. Perry VH, Holmes C. Microglial priming in neurodegenerative disease. *Nature Reviews Neurology*. 2014;10:217–224.

59. Morris GP, Clark IA, Zinn R, Vissel B. Microglia: a new frontier for synaptic plasticity, learning and memory, and neurodegenerative disease research. *Neurobiology of Learning and Memory*. 2013;105:40–53.

60. Raison CL, Dantzer R, Kelley KW, et al. CSF concentrations of brain tryptophan and kynurenines during immune stimulation with IFN-α: relationship to CNS immune responses and depression. *Molecular Psychiatry*. 2010;15:393–403.

61. Maes M, Bosmans E, De Jongh R, Kenis G, Vandoolaeghe E, Neels H. Increased serum IL-6 and IL-1 receptor antagonist concentrations in major depression and treatment resistant depression. *Cytokine*. 1997;9:853–858.

Chapter 6

62. Das UN. Is obesity an inflammatory condition? *Nutrition*. 2001;17:953–966.

63. Luppino FS, de Wit LM, Bouvy PF, et al. Overweight, obesity, and depression: a systematic review and meta-analysis of longitudinal studies. *Archives of General Psychiatry*. 2010;67:220–229.

64. Chung HY, Cesari M, Anton S, et al. Molecular inflammation: underpinnings of aging and age-related diseases. *Ageing Research Reviews*. 2009;8:18–30.

65. Dopico XC, Evangelou M, Ferreira RC, et al. Widespread seasonal gene expression reveals annual differences in human immunity and physiology. *Nature Communications*. 2015;6:7000.

66. Kendler KS, Thornton LM, Gardner CO. Stressful life events and previous episodes in the etiology of major depression in women. *American Journal of Psychiatry*. 2000;157:1243–1251.

67. Mazure CM. Life stressors as risk factors in depression. *Clinical Psychology: Science and Practice*. 1998;5:291–313.

68. Kendler KS, Hettema JM, Butera F, Gardner CO, Prescott CA. Life event

dimensions of loss, humiliation, entrapment and danger in the prediction of onsets of major depression and generalized anxiety. *Archives of General Psychiatry.* 2003;60:789–796.

69. Boyle PJ, Feng Z, Raab GM. Does widowhood increase mortality risk? Testing for selection effects by comparing causes of spousal death. *Epidemiology.* 2011;22:1–5.

70. Carey IM, Shah SM, DeWilde S, Harris T, Victor CR, Cook DG. Increased risk of acute cardiovascular events after partner bereavement: a matched cohort study. *JAMA Internal Medicine.* 2014;174:598–605.

71. Wohleb ES, Franklin T, Iwata M, Duman RS. Integrating neuroimmune systems in the neurobiology of depression. *Nature Reviews Neuroscience.* 2016;17:497–511.

72. Reader BF, Jarrett BL, McKim DB, Wohleb ES, Godbout JP, Sheridan JF. Peripheral and central effects of repeated social defeat stress: monocyte trafficking, microglial activation, and anxiety. *Neuroscience.* 2015;289:429–442.

73. Schultze-Florey CR, Martínez-Maza O, Magpantay L, et al. When grief makes you sick: Bereavement induced systemic inflammation is a question of genotype. *Brain, Behavior, and Immunity.* 2012;26:1066–1071.

74. Glaser R, Kiecolt-Glaser JK. Stress-induced immune dysfunction: implications for health. *Nature Reviews Immunology.* 2005;5:243–251.

75. Bellingrath S, Rohleder N, Kudielka BM. Effort-reward-imbalance in healthy teachers is associated with higher LPS-stimulated production and lower glucocorticoid sensitivity of interleukin-6 in vitro. *Biological Psychology.* 2013;92:403–409.

76. Kiecolt-Glaser JK, Derry HM, Fagundes CP. Inflammation: depression fans the flames and feasts on the heat. *American Journal of Psychiatry.* 2015;172:1075–1091.

77. Cohen IV, Makunts T, Atayee R, Abagyan R. Population scale data reveals the antidepressant effects of ketamine and other therapeutics approved for non-psychiatric indications. *Scientific Reports.* 2017;7:1450.

78. Darwin C, Prodger P. *The Expression of the Emotions in Man and Animals.* USA: Oxford University Press; 1998.

79. Psychiatric Genetics Consortium. Genome-wide association analyses identify 44 risk variants and refine the genetic architecture of major depressive disorder. *bioRxiv.* 2017.

80. Liu W, Yan M, Liu Y, et al. Olfactomedin 4 down-regulates innate immunity against Helicobacter pylori infection. *Proceedings of the National Academy of Sciences.* 2010;107:11056–11061.

Chapter 7

81. Lee CG, Carr MC, Murdoch SJ, et al. Adipokines, inflammation, and visceral adiposity across the menopausal transition: a prospective study. *The Journal of Clinical Endocrinology & Metabolism.* 2009;94:1104–1110.

82. Chang CK, Hayes RD, Perera G, et al. Life expectancy at birth for people with serious mental illness and other major disorders from a secondary mental health care case register in London. *PLoS ONE.* 2011;6:p.e19590.

83. Nordentoft M, Wahlbeck K, Hällgren J, et al. Excess mortality, causes of death and life expectancy in 270,770 patients with recent onset of mental disorders in Denmark, Finland and Sweden. *PLoS ONE.* 2013;8:p.e55176.

84. Miller G. Is pharma running out of brainy ideas? *Science.* 2010;329:502–504.

85. Arrowsmith J, Harrison R. Drug repositioning: the business case and current strategies to repurpose shelved candidates and marketed drugs. In: Barratt MJ, Frail DE, eds. *Drug repositioning: Bringing new life to shelved assets and existing drugs.* Hoboken, NJ: John Wiley & Sons, Inc.; 2012:9–31.

86. Köhler O, Benros ME, Nordentoft M, et al. Effect of anti-inflammatory treatment on depression, depressive symptoms, and adverse effects: a systematic review and meta-analysis of randomized clinical trials. *JAMA Psychiatry.* 2014;71:1381–1391.

87. Kappelmann N, Lewis G, Dantzer R, Jones PB, Khandaker GM. Antidepressant activity of anti-cytokine treatment: a systematic review and meta-analysis of clinical trials of chronic inflammatory conditions. *Molecular Psychiatry.* 2016.

88. Wittenberg G, Stylianou A, Zhang Y, et al. A mega-analysis of immuno-modulatory drug effects on depressive symptoms. *bioRxiv.* 2018.

89. Raison CL, Rutherford RE, Woolwin BJ, et al. A randomised controlled trial of the tumor necrosis factor antagonist infliximab for treatment-resistant depression: the role of baseline inflammatory markers. *JAMA Psychiatry.* 2013;70:31–41.

90. Groves DA, Brown VJ. Vagal nerve stimulation: a review of its applications and potential mechanisms that mediate its clinical effects. *Neuroscience and Biobehavioral Reviews.* 2005;29:493–500.

91. Fox D. The electric cure. *Nature.* 2017;545:20–22.

92. Creswell JD, Irwin MR, Burklund LJ, et al. Mindfulness-based stress reduction training reduces loneliness and pro-inflammatory gene expression in older adults: a small randomized controlled trial. *Brain, Behavior, and Immunity.* 2012;26:1095–1101.

93. Bower JE, Irwin MR. Mind–body therapies and control of inflammatory

biology: a descriptive review. *Brain, Behavior, and Immunity.* 2016;51:1–11.

94. Maurer K, Volk S, Gerbaldo H. Auguste D and Alzheimer's disease. *The Lancet.* 1997;349:1546–1549.

95. Tuppo EE, Arias HR. The role of inflammation in Alzheimer's disease. *The International Journal of Biochemistry & Cell Biology.* 2005;37:289–305.

96. McGeer PL, McGeer EG. Inflammation and the degenerative diseases of aging. *Annals of the New York Academy of Sciences.* 2004;1035:104–116.

97. Guerreiro R, Wojtas A, Bras J, et al. *TREM2* variants in Alzheimer's disease. *New England Journal of Medicine.* 2013;368:117–127.

98. Kraepelin E, Diefendorf AR. *Clinical psychiatry: a text-book for students and physicians.* London: Macmillan; 1915.

99. Noll R. Kraepelin's "lost biological psychiatry"? Auto-intoxication, organotherapy and surgery for dementa praecox. *History of Psychiatry.* 2007;18:301–320.

100. Psychiatric Genetics Consortium. Biological insights from 108 schizophrenia-associated genetic loci. *Nature.* 2014;511:421–427.

101. Sekar A, Bialas AR, de Rivera H, et al. Schizophrenia risk from complex variation of complement component 4. *Nature.* 2016;530:177–183.

102. Davies G, Welham J, Chant D, Torrey EF, McGrath J. A systematic review and meta-analysis of Northern Hemisphere season of birth studies in schizophrenia. *Schizophrenia Bulletin.* 2003;29:587–593.

103. Khandaker GM, Cousins L, Deakin J, Lennox BR, Yolken R, Jones PB. Inflammation and immunity in schizophrenia: implications for pathophysiology and treatment. *The Lancet Psychiatry.* 2015;2:258–270.

104. Zandi MS, Irani SR, Lang B, et al. Disease-relevant autoantibodies in first episode schizophrenia. *Journal of Neurology.* 2011;258:686–688.

Acknowledgements

I would like to thank many colleagues, too many to name, in academia, industry and the NHS, for all their help in teaching me to think differently about depression and about how we might develop new treatments in future.

I would particularly like to thank several people who were kind enough to read an early version of this book: Matthew d'Ancona, Simon Baron-Cohen, Claire Brough, Amelia Bullmore, Jeremy Bullmore, Paul Higgins, Peter Jones, Golam Khandaker, Trevor Robbins, Lorinda Turner, Petra Vértes and Jeremy Vine.

I am very grateful to Rebecca Nicolson, Aurea Carpenter and Catherine Gibbs at Short Books for making it into a book; Emma Craigie for copy editing; and Helena Maxwell for her illustrations.

But it would not have been done without my wife, Mary Pitt, who got me started and helped me see it through in many ways.

Disclaimers

The views and opinions expressed in this book are those of the author solely. Likewise any unintended factual errors are my responsibility alone.

I regret that I am not in a position to offer professional advice to readers of this book concerning their personal experiences of mental or physical health disorders.

Index

Professor Edward Bullmore BA MB PhD FRCP FRCPsych FMedSci trained in medicine at the University of Oxford and then at St Bartholomew's Hospital in London. After working as a physician in the University of Hong Kong, he trained as a psychiatrist at St George's Hospital, the Bethlem Royal and the Maudsley Hospital in London, and as a clinical scientist at the Institute of Psychiatry, King's College London. Since 1999, he has been a Professor of Psychiatry at the University of Cambridge, where he is now Head of the Department of Psychiatry and Director of the Wolfson Brain Imaging Centre in the Department of Clinical Neurosciences. He is an honorary consultant psychiatrist and Director of Research and Development for Cambridgeshire and Peterborough NHS Foundation Trust. Since 2005, he has also worked half-time for GlaxoSmithKline and is currently leading an academic-industrial consortium for the development of new anti-inflammatory drugs for depression. He is a world expert in neuroscience and mental health.